WOMEN on WHEELS

The Scandalous Untold Histories of Women in Bicycling

APRIL STREETER

Microcosm Publishing
Portland, OR

WOMEN ON WHEELS: The Scandalous Untold Histories of Women in Bicycling

Part of the Bicycling Revolution Series
© April Streeter, 2021
This edition © Microcosm Publishing, 2021
Illustrated by Matt Gauck and Lindsey Cleworth
First published April 13, 2021

For a catalog, write or visit:
Microcosm Publishing
2752 N Williams Ave.
Portland, OR 97227
www.Microcosm.Pub

ISBN 978-1-62106-207-3
This is Microcosm #227
Cover illustration by Lindsey Cleworth

To join the ranks of high-class stores that feature Microcosm titles, talk to your local rep: In the U.S. **Como** (Atlantic), **Fujii** (Midwest), **Travelers West** (Pacific), **Brunswick** in Canada, **Turnaround** in Europe, **New South** in Australia and New Zealand, and **Baker & Taylor Publisher Services** in Asia, India, and South Africa. We are sold in the gift market by **Gifts of Nature** and by **Faire**.

Did you know that you can buy our books directly from us at sliding scale rates? Support a small, independent publisher and pay less than Amazon's price at **www.Microcosm.Pub**

Library of Congress Cataloging-in-Publication Data

Names: Streeter, April, author.
Title: Women on wheels : the scandalous untold histories of women in
    bicycling / April Streeter.
Description: Second edition. | Portland : Microcosm Publishing, [2021] |
    Summary: "A feminist history of bicycling for sport and adventure spans
    a century of women who changed the world from two wheels. This vivacious
    tale, peppered with fascinating details from primary sources, shows how
    women were sometimes the stars of bicycle races and exhibitions, and
    other times had to overcome sexism, exclusion, and economic inequalities
    in order to ride. From the almost burlesque show races and creative
    performances of the 19th century to the evolution of cycling as a modern
    sport and form of transportation, April Streeter brings her exuberant
    eye for character, fashion, and story to convey the evolving emotional
    resonance of bicycling for women and their communities. Interweaving
    pedal-powered history with profiles of bicyclists who made their mark,
    like Katharine Hepburn, Annie Londonderry, Kittie Knox, Dorothy
    Lawrence, Louise Armaindo, and more"-- Provided by publisher.
Identifiers: LCCN 2020050509 | ISBN 9781621062073 (paperback)
Subjects: LCSH: Cycling--United States--History--19th century. |
    Cycling--United States--History--20th century. | Women cyclists--United
    States--History--19th century. | Women cyclists--United
    States--History--20th century. | Discrimination in sports--United
    States--History--19th century. | Discrimination in sports--United
    States--History--20th century.
Classification: LCC GV1045 .S83 2021 | DDC 796.6082--dc23
LC record available at https://lccn.loc.gov/2020050509

MICROCOSM · PUBLISHING

Microcosm Publishing is Portland's most diversified publishing house and distributor with a focus on the colorful, authentic, and empowering. Our books and zines have put your power in your hands since 1996, equipping readers to make positive changes in their lives and in the world around them. Microcosm emphasizes skill-building, showing hidden histories, and fostering creativity through challenging conventional publishing wisdom with books and bookettes about DIY skills, food, bicycling, gender, self-care, and social justice. What was once a distro and record label was started by Joe Biel in his bedroom and has become among the oldest independent publishing houses in Portland, OR. We are a politically moderate, centrist publisher in a world that has inched to the right for the past 80 years.

Global labor conditions are bad, and our roots in industrial Cleveland in the 70s and 80s made us appreciate the need to treat workers right. Therefore, our books are MADE IN THE USA.

CONTENTS

INTRODUCTION

When We're All Bicyclists

In 2010, after living in Sweden for five years, I looked forward to returning to "my" bicycle town of Portland, Oregon. As a freelance journalist and blogger who was also car free, a bicycle had been my preferred mobility mode to interviews and events for years. Once back in Portland, however, I felt a reverse bicycle culture shock. By that year the stream of people in the bike lanes of this famously bikeable, midsize West coast city was about one-third female. The feeling in those lanes on my commutes, however, felt distinctly male. The bike-lane *zeitgeist* seemed to me to be saying "Go faster, get aggressive... be a cyclist." I just wanted to be a person who bikes. Why did biking feel so different—much more aggressive, and less safe—when compared to biking in the midsize Scandinavian city I'd just left?

That was the question I started researching. I'd already been reporting and blogging about sustainable transport for years, so I knew about many of the ways U.S. women differed from men in their willingness and desire to bike in city traffic.

Yet what I uncovered as I researched back through the bicycle history was that the narrative about women and biking had been guided by men, especially in the early decades of the bike.

The simplified story went something like this: 1895. "Safety" bicycle is introduced, with drop frame, chain, pneumatic tires. An explosion of female cyclists, all dressed in bloomers, follows. The true tale, of course, is much richer, more complex, and not so straightforward. It is stocked with circus characters, female daredevils and courageous racers, plus quite a few women who simply recognized "bike joy." These women yearned to ride before the safety bike and in spite of the constant oversight from men trying to control their purse strings, their outfits, and their sexuality.

Digging for and finding a hidden wealth of historical bicycle heroines was fun, and though sometimes sad, always inspiring. Together with the research and reporting I did on the hurdles contemporary women in the U.S. faced when using a bike for transportation, I put together a guide, titled *Women on Wheels: A Handbook and How-To For City Cyclists*. Self published in 2012, this volume interspersed advice on how to be a happy year-round bike commuter with short vignettes of many of the women I discovered.

Even as I sold out that first volume I knew I wanted to delve deeper into the social history of women and biking. There were women's stories I had obsessed over—Kittie Knox, Louise Armaindo—and wanted to know more about. I also wanted to piece together a narrative that helped better explain how bicycle marketing through the decades had included and excluded different groups from the joy of biking.

The result is what you are now reading.

Through the research and the writing, my goal has been to continue to see myself and other humans as not just specific types of cyclists, although of course types and tribes do exist, but rather as people who bike. As this is a social history-of the hundred years from roughly 1868-1970, it doesn't take the more nuanced approach to gender that a study of more recent bicycle history would. It is interesting to imagine, though, how some of the stronger racing and endurance bicyclists of yore would identify now.

As a bike advocate and bike ride leader, my interest is also to spread the joy of biking in all its many forms. For myself, biking has changed as I've changed. At three, I was a happy tricyclist on a candy-apple red three wheeler. By eight years old I enjoyed a Big Wheel and endless careening down the hill in front of our California bungalow. At eleven I received the most popular bike of the era—a Schwinn with a copper-colored frame and sparkles embedded in its white banana-shaped saddle—and got my first taste of the bike's ability to give a preteen freedom to roam.

At twenty I loved a boy who tried and failed to make me into a road cyclist. Then, after almost a decade of not riding I experienced a bicycle rebirth when I married a Swede. My partner and I weren't cyclists—we just biked. We biked because bicycles were faster than walking and more fun than the bus. When we had two sons we biked as a family because it still seemed more fun to strap them into the Burley trailer than into car seats.

In spite of my experiences as a bicyclist, I still feel embarrassed sometimes that I'm not a *cyclist*. I don't have road bikes in the shed. I might never do a century. My adventures traveling by bike are mostly slow urban crawls. But bicycling still gives me a feeling of freedom that is hard to describe.

Stories tell it better. Stories of women, in long skirts or short skirts or no skirts at all, on tall bikes or small ones, striving for something that is hard to articulate—self-agency, self-determination, control. In biking, I think all of us seek release from the "to-do list" and a reconnection with the natural world that seems easy on two (or three) wheels.

There are so many stories out there, more tales than I can tell here. Most of my narratives center on women in North America, and even with geographical limits I can't capture all the good stories. I do hope to have put together enough material to expand the perspective around womens' role in the social history of the bicycle.

Looking to the past I found so many more women biking than I could ever have imagined—courageous women who broke down barriers and made it easier for many of us to enjoy the ride. Looking to the future, in my perfect world we'll all have wheels and agency to ride—we'll all be bicyclists.

In olden times the woman rode

As fitted one of subject mind:

Her lord and master sat before,

She on a pillion sat behind.

But now upon her flying wheel,

She holds her independent way,

And when she rides a race with man,

'Tis even chance she wins the day.

—John Galsworthy (1867–1933)

CHAPTER ONE

BY PEARSALL BROS.

Invention, or Life on Two Wheels (1818-1870)

Earliest Models

Men created the bicycle. That's the official narrative. Behind the scenes, wives and sisters, housekeepers and housemaids, friends and lovers contributed to the early bicycle's development and innovation with their supportive labor, and possibly their suggestions. We might never know the full scale of their contributions. We do know that in spite of many hurdles and restrictions, women wasted little time in using even the first bicycles for social and cultural change. And for joy.

Baron Karl de Drais was a German inventor who designed one of the forerunners of the modern bike in the early 1800s. de Drais was an inventor and a civil servant forest manager, and he may have been solving a personal transport problem. The result of de Drais' tinkering, which he called the *laufmaschine* or "running machine" was eventually christened the draisine. It may have been based on an earlier horse-free wheeled contraption attributed to Frenchman Mede de Sivrac and called the célérifere. De Drais' invention was variously dubbed the hobby horse, swift walker, and—my favorite—the "dandy charger." This pre-bicycle looked, from the side, like an oxen yoke, with forks curving down to fore and aft wheels. It had a rudimentary steering bar and required riders to rest their pelvises on the middle of the yoke's long beam and scoot forward, one foot at a time. Awkward, yes, but de Drais' contraption didn't require either hay or a barn, and going downhill, a rider could achieve speeds of nearly ten miles per hour.

Somewhere in England, some smart woman may have seen a "dandy" on his charger and yearned to ride the contraption. Quite possibly it was even Mary Newman, wife of British entrepreneur Denis Johnson. In 1818, Johnson was selling dandy chargers, and fashioned a woman's version. Johnson called his female-friendly contraption the "anti-straddling" hobby horse. Its low center bar would allow women to easily step over and onto it, even wearing a floor-skimming skirt. A higher, center-bar version with a cushioned seat called the "Lady's Accelerator" and designed by London's Hancock & Co. was advertised in 1820.

Unfortunately these models were never mass-produced. They weren't practical or ergonomic enough and their prices were out of reach for most people. Soon the novelty of this early spurt of personal locomotion via dandy horses fizzled out.

Behind the scenes, though, the Baron's invention inspired additional tinkerers around Europe to slowly innovate the draisine forward in the direction of the bicycle we now know. An important next set of improvements was initiated by blacksmith Pierre Michaux, his son Ernest and their partner Pierre Lallemont, resulting in the velocipede (from the Latin *veloc* for "swift" and *ped* for "foot") also referred to as a "boneshaker" for its lack of rider comforts like a soft saddle or shock absorbers. Heavy and iron-framed, with forward-motion axle-crank pedals directly driving the front wheel, the velocipede sparked a frenzy of riding from 1868 to 1870.

This frenzy swept along quite a few women in its wake.

Miss America

I t took women almost no time to become adept at the heavy, clunky velocipedes. By November 1868, a group of women raced a distance of 500 meters (one-third of a mile) on the boulevards of Bordeaux. That race was memorialized first in a pencil sketch in the French *Le Monde Illustre*, and then copied in America's *Harper's* magazine, with one significant and telling difference. In the American illustration the women's shins are covered with billowing petticoats not seen in the *Le Monde* sketch. Studious Harper's readers might have realized how dangerous those petticoats would be to actual pedaling.

Author Hugh Dancey, in his book *French Cycling, A Social and Cultural History*, says these early women racers were referred to in the press as "les dames bordelaises"[1] because of their provenance from Bordeaux, and most likely many of them were working-class women who chanced upon this attention-getting occupational sideline. They participated in staged races that may have been as much about showing off bared calves and skimpy costumes (one observer described the girl cyclists as "coquettishly rigged as pages") as they were about advancing womens' rights to bicycle.[2] Newspaper reports also had young women competing in velocipede races in the Parisian Bois de Boulogne park in 1868.

By the autumn of 1869, wooden-and-iron framed velocipedes were at the height of their French, English, and also their American popularity. A trio of bicycle-loving French brothers—Aimé, Marius, and René Olivier— worked with Michaux et Cie, a new velocipede company, to help finance mass production. As a marketing aid, René Olivier decided to organize one of the very first long-distance velocipede races between Rouen and Paris, a distance of 123 kilometers (76 miles), on the 7th of November.

Over questionable roads, with no gears and zero shock absorbers on their velocipedes (and definitely no support and gear "SAG" wagons) contestants were expected to pedal as fast as they could between the two cities. More than 100 cyclists showed up for the challenge, competing for a new velocipede and 1,000 francs in prize money. Depending on the source consulted, either four or five women were among the contestants.

Many in the French public were already acquainted with women racing bikes, though there was stigma attached to those who became racers. Women in the mid-to-late 1800s were still constricted by the mores and morals of the time. In addition, they were constrained by confining underwear and outerwear, many had heavy housework and mothering duties, and all remained hampered by physicians' admonitions that athletic activity like biking would a) damage their wombs, making them inferior baby machines, or b) over sexualize them, mainly by allowing masturbation via bicycle saddles.

From actual demonstration, it was clear that women of average limberness and strength could pedal on two wheels. But it was equally clear that select moralists saw the bicycle as a dangerous vehicle of empowerment, and so there was a tendency for the mainstream to preach and protest each time women vied for freedoms similar to those the male velocipedists enjoyed. And women not only riding, but *racing*! That always and particularly inflamed the senses of naysayers, raising hackles while causing the pencils of caricaturists to work furiously.

Because of this, it is not surprising that the only female recorded as finishing that first long-distance velocipede race organized by René Olivier entered under the mysterious moniker "Miss America."

Who was Miss America? Sources suggest she was the wife of Rowley B. Turner, an enterprising salesperson for the Coventry Sewing Machine company who wholeheartedly embraced cycling and cycle racing. Rowley Turner was British, but as the Paris-based agent of Coventry he had brought home a velocipede from France in 1868 and convinced his boss (also his uncle) that there was enough of an expanding market to start to manufacture velocipedes in Britain and then export them back to France. But his timing wasn't great. With the coming of the Franco-Prussian war, by 1870 French trade in bicycles and enthusiasm for biking stalled. Turner pivoted, and in a twist, marketed the machines at home in Britain as "Velocipèdes Américains." The French had had an edge in velocipede adaptation, and perhaps Turner added the "Américains" as a branding flourish; after all, there was always an aura of freedom connected with the American experiment.

Rowley Turner's success at convincing Coventry to manufacture velocipedes played a key role in facilitating British bicycle innovation and a new industry. James Starley, a foreman at Coventry and a talented inventor, was allowed to turn his focus to bikes. Starley enthusiastically began improving upon the French model. He helped usher in the next era of biking with his small back wheel/huge front wheel cycle design, which after 1870 was dubbed the Ordinary.

As is frequently the case, while Rowley B. Turner gets a footnote in bicycle history, Mrs. Turner is listed only as "E. Turner" in her husband Rowley's 1871 Census entry. Author David Herlihy said her real name was Elisabeth Sarti and she was born in Lyon in 1847.[3] She probably chose to race under cover of the Miss America moniker to avoid possible criticism or damage to her husband's livelihood. In the official record of race finishers, she came in 29th, right ahead of Mr. Turner at 30th.

In his seminal work *The Bicycle,* Herlihy said Miss America was described as petite and a "fierce competitor" who continued to race and managed to take first place in a mixed gender 1870 competition in Rouen. In Herlihy's account, Miss America overnighted by train to the town of Blois where she dispensed "with the local competition with embarrassing ease."[4]

By the spring of 1869, "fair correspondents" in the United States were inquiring in the *New York Evening Herald* where they could find velocipede riding academies. A little later that same year it was Boston that became the first US city to provide American women with a place to learn to pedal the velocipede, with "French" machines and special dressing rooms. Unfortunately, Boston was also the first city, just a year later in 1870, to stymie cyclists with a law against sidewalk riding. Because the roads were few and bad, this simple injunction was part of the boneshaker fever's end. Also, after just two years, there seemed already to be a division in women's bicycling: a rift developed, at least in the minds of the male newspaper writers, between so-called demure females who dressed as modestly as possible when trying out the freedom of the wheel, and those that took bigger risks with their bike fashion and received more judgment and censure from the press.

Englishwoman Cora Pearl fell in the latter category—a risk taker. The *Dictionary of National Biography* from 1895[5] said she was one of sixteen children, born in 1836 to musical producer Frederick Crouch and his singer wife Lydia Pearson. Her birth name was Eliza Emma Crouch.

Taking the name of Cora Pearl at around the age of 20, Crouch became a part-time courtesan, and an actress and daring provocateur, playing Cupid in a barely-there dress[6] in a theatrical production at the Haymarket theatre in London. She achieved further notoriety in the English press for her choice of French lovers, establishing herself in

Parisian society by 1860 and appearing in scanty costumes during horse rides in the Parisian park known as the Bois de Boulogne. In photos Cora always appeared alluring and with a sparkle. She was described as an excellent horsewoman, though otherwise descriptions of her style and fashion were generally judgmental and negative.

Cora was up for anything, it seemed, and something of an exhibitionist. In the summer of 1868 newspapers reported that she was riding a velocipede in men's clothing and wearing a bright red wig. She may have been outrageous, but she was also a trend setter. In June of that year, to explain why the fashionable aristocracy in Paris abandoned biking in the Bois to instead ride on the Allee des Acacias, the *New York Daily Herald* claimed simply, "It is Cora Pearl's fault." "The most determined female innovator," the newspaper continued, "having gotten tired of driving ponies, propelled herself and sat to advantage astride a velocipede."[7]

As a courtesan Cora was dependent on her lovers for generous financial gifts and was able to purchase properties and continue living extravagantly. In the memoir she wrote shortly before her death she related that she was accustomed to riding her velocipede near one of her homes in Maisons-Laffitte, a fashionable and expensive Parisian suburb.

Cora's exploits went on—she gained and lost fortunes, had affairs with princes, and spent quite a bit of time in court for refusing to pay her bills. The French aristocracy was shocked by Cora's brazenness, but didn't seem put off by her biking, perhaps because the French were more open-minded when it came to the idea of letting women ride and more tolerant of accompanying fashion adaptations. In addition to the French being first to stage women's velocipede races—which were more entertainment and spectacle than a serious sports exercise—the French Empress Eugenie was said to be "partial" to bicycle exercise and was observed taking rides in the park and long excursions into the country on her "mechanical steed."[8]

Cora and her French contemporary Blanche D'Antigny, born in 1840, flaunted convention in many ways to make money and achieve a measure of freedom, and their bicycle riding could be viewed as part of that quest. Blanche, birth name Marie Ernestine Antigny, was a singer, actress, and portrait model. Both Blanche and Cora were also *demi-mondaines*, or mistresses, kept women who collected financial favors from wealthy lovers and doled out sexual favors in return.

Blanche had run away from her home at fourteen, taken various lovers, and ended up in Paris, posing for artist Paul Baudry for the well-known painting *Penitent Magdalene*. Author Emile Zola also used her as inspiration for his novel *Nana*. And Blanche's bike riding was commemorated along with a gorgeous velocipede in an oil painting first thought to be the work of artist Betinet but now attributed to the artist Henri de L'etang[9]. Blanche's smart outfit in the portrait consisted of a somber gray jacket, long and cinched at the waist, fitted over maroon pantaloons, and accompanied by tall black boots. Her outfit wasn't that different from a riding habit of the 1860s, just scantier. The velocipede generally required a running—or at the least, leaning against something—start, making the pantaloons something of a necessity.

Neither Cora nor Blanche came to a particularly happy end. In 1874, Blanche died at 37 after being infected with typhoid in Egypt; Cora's fortune declined with the Second Empire's crumbling in France, and she was engulfed in a scandal (not the first) after her lover lost his fortune due in part to her profligate spending and gambling. She published her memoirs in 1886 in a tell-all book that flustered some members of the French and English aristocracies, before she died the same year. Obituaries described her as being seen at the Paris Grand Prix horse races a year before her death completely robbed of health, decrepit, leaning on a cane and looking ravaged by time, with a "horrible, corpse-like face." She was 50.[10]

What to Wear on a Velocipede

Because the velocipede era was relatively short, women barely had time to figure out what fashions would work a-wheel before these early bikes themselves went out of fashion. A few intrepid riders managed to get at least a few revolutions of the wheel during what the press called "velocipede fever." A Google search on the terms "velocipede" and "ladies" turns up scores of short mentions. In the United States, manufacturing firm Pickering and Davis designed velocipedes for the home market including the Pickering ladies' velocipede, which had a sweet, comfy-looking basket seat and a slightly lower step-through frame than their other velocipedes. Pickering and Davis also published the short-lived magazine *The Velocipedist*, which seemed to take a positive view of women riding. The magazine declared in March 1869 that "active" young women "do not see why they should be denied the exercise and amusement the bicycle so abundantly furnishes." A Miss Pearsall, the Misses Addie Scarcey and Libbie Francis, plus a matron named Mrs. Jennie Peterson, all managed to get a few lines in *The Velocipedist* for their "graceful" riding.

And grace is great, of course—admirable. Who wouldn't want to pull off gracefulness on a heavy iron-and-wood contraption that could easily eat your skirt and thus throw you to the ground? In the early bicycle era, however, the word "grace" was something of a dog whistle. It meant you were acceptable—not too far outside the decorous norm. A graceful rider was assumed to not only handle her wheel but also be modestly dressed, be ladylike. Men didn't get to be graceful. And neither did show-offs like Cora Pearl and Blanche d'Antigny.

If you wanted grace you could not put on a pair of pants and hop on a wheel. Instead, a look at the illustrations of the day showed a slight shortening of skirts and petticoats and the addition of loose and roomy pantaloons so that ankles were still demurely covered; or, taking a (riskier) Blanche d'Antigny approach with a shorter skirt, pantaloons and then tight shin-showing leggings tucked into boots.

But what if you couldn't or didn't want to manage flapping skirts while cranking the pedals? A few women eager to ride the velocipede might have resorted to putting on a pair of knickers and passing as a boy. This would certainly be a more comfortable way to ride, and not so difficult physically for slim young girls or women who could easily access their brothers' or cousins' wardrobes–although hiding long hair was an issue. In the very first volume of *The Velocipedist* from February 1869 the editorialists proposed that American ladies *should* be able to ride, but with the difficulty of the era's fashions, many were likely to have decided, like Jessica in the Merchant of Venice, to obscure themselves "in the lovely garnish of a boy."[11]

If there were women who donned the "garnish" of a boy in order to ride the velocipede, their stories have yet to be widely discovered. The idea of the tomboy had already made it into the culture by the 1860s, but even if a young girl might be allowed to be more adventurous and less proper in her behavior and fashions, by the middle of their teen years young women were expected to let their skirts down and put their long hair up. As we'll see, the risk of reputational damage followed women throughout the decades. And this difficulty—reputation versus freedom— would be women's dilemma right up to the present, balancing between the personally practical and what is deemed acceptable. We are still taught to dress for others, still apt to be judged harshly if we don't get it quite right in society's eyes.

Before the velocipede era completely faded, a slight amount of outfit assistance came in the form of the pastimes of archery, roller skating, and ice skating. Athleticism in women was a new phenomenon and still on cultural trial. But a search for fitting exercise for women stemmed from the worry that (white) women were languishing due to restrictive clothing and few means to exercise. Through the ages lone female outliers had of course demonstrated athletic skill and endurance, probably more than we know. And brown and black women were expected to have—though not admired for—strength and stamina. In white society, apart from horse skills (side saddle, no straddle), athletic skill and endurance from middle and upper class white women had been generally considered unseemly. But doctors had become more aware that young (again, white) women suffered a host of ailments that could be cured with exercise and fresh air. So they tentatively endorsed the growing popularity of archery, ice skating, and then roller skating, which helped in turn to lower the barriers that separated males and females in athletic skill and endeavor. And though controversial, the walking sport known as pedestrianism intensified the need for less restrictive fashions for women: less length and weight in skirts and petticoats, slightly looser corsets. As bicycle culture advanced, the outfits devised for these other sports activities would spur some innovations and inspiration for what women might wear while bicycling.

Carrie Moore, Skatorial Queen

Carrie Moore, also called the Skatorial Queen, first flaunted her innate athletic prowess on ice skates. Born Caroline Augusta Moore in 1840, Carrie was a native of the fairly progressive burg of Concord, Massachusetts. Moore was naturally gifted on anything with wheels or blades. She gave exhibitions of both her roller skating and her ice skating in colorful, yet demure outfits that featured big skirts but showed a bit of ankle. Concord became a big velocipede town in the late 1860s and when the fever hit, Carrie Moore made a bold move. She bought herself a custom-made velocipede.

'The Concord Skater" as Carrie was also known, was famously limber and learned to master the velocipede in no time. She began to appear in small towns and then larger ones, displaying her skills at trick riding. She was mostly, though not always, well received by her audiences, and she developed a good sense of how to stay on the respectable side, in her performances and her outfits.

Trick velocipede riding had by then invaded the circuses, and women doing fabulous feats on two wheels wasn't uncommon, but circus performers also weren't considered polite society. Carrie had to take care not to be compared to women like Ella Zuila, an Australian funambulist who perfected riding a velocipede along a high wire. Ella wore plunging necklines and sequined, one-piece outfits that were actually practical for her line of work but were called scandalous by the press. Those body-hugging suits weren't anything Carrie Moore dared wear.

In 1869, Moore took her velocipede show on tour. In one of her first performances, her outfit consisted of a blue tunic that covered everything except face and hands, yet was "fitting the body very closely" as the *New Orleans Crescent* put it.[12] The tunic had a modesty skirt underneath it and underneath that a pair of loose red trunks that revealed a tiny slice of flesh-colored tights. On her head she sported a matching blue hat with a waving ostrich plume.

In this ensemble Carrie toured from town to town. She advanced her skills, and made trick velocipede riding look a lot easier than it actually was. "Carrie Moore, the velocipede performer, picks up two chairs, one in each hand, while riding, and carries them around the room; makes eights and curves without use of hands; makes a circuit of the room without the use of hand or feet; stands on one foot on the saddle, and performs the feat of passing the hoop over the head and manages to get it through [sic] while riding Mexican fashion."[13]

By 1870 Carrie made it as far west as Portland, Oregon, with her velocipede act. The velocipede craze had lost velocity. Heavy, cumbersome, uncomfortable, and expensive–it's a wonder velocipedes ever became as popular as they did. Velocipedes were never in more than modest production, and their cost, between $75 and $125, was many months of a working man's salary. Clearly, humans were eager for the excitement of personal forward motion. The velocipede had pedals a rider cranked around and around to drive the front wheel forward, making human-powered motion a more interesting idea when compared to the awkward walking motion the pedalless draisine required. But the velocipede suffered the same short curve of popularity as the draisine–first the early enthusiasts, the short mainstream craze, and then a precipitous decline. In the velocipede's case, the global boom to bust happened over three short years.

Ultimately the main obstacle was civic. Shortly into the velo's first season, cities drafted the first injunctions against sidewalk riding. Horse and cart drivers hated the interlopers, and once cities outlawed the sidewalks, it was like a death knell for velocipedes.

Aristocrats and the well-off moved on to the next pastime. Thus, after returning from Portland, Carrie Moore went back to skating and married her manager Charles Lovett in 1872. He adopted her last name of "Moore" and they toured together, giving roller skating performances for a few more years. She died in Concord in 1892.

CHAPTER TWO

Women Take The Wheel
(1870-1888)

Another way to look at the velocepide's demise is simply as the inevitable result of a product delivery lag between bicycle 1.0 and the next upgrade. The velocipede was a mediocre first generation as far as usability was concerned. By 1870, however, British innovators were already laying the foundation for a bigger bicycle industry, and the Americans also had lots of designers, developers, and manufacturers eager to get in on this new offshoot of the machine age. In England, James Starley was innovating a new and faster kind of bicycle inside the old sewing machine factory at Coventry. Starley's genius was to enlarge the velocipede's front wheel, allowing the gearless machines to go faster, while shrinking the back wheel significantly.

An entire industry of engineers and manufacturers built up around the Coventry Machine Co. (as it was called after switching much of its production from sewing machines to bicycles), and in other parts of Britain. The British get much credit for early bicycle innovation, and English riders continued to also advance bicycle racing. In the U.S., round two of cycling mania took a little longer, getting in gear in the mid 1870s once Colonel Albert Pope started to manufacture "high-wheel" machines at Columbia Bicycles outside of Boston.

Popular though they were becoming, high-wheeled bikes were also controversial. There were real risks of riders easily taking a header over the handlebars when meeting with the smallest of impediments in the road. Sharing the road was still an issue. The high-wheel bike, also called the "Ordinary" after an early model name, were at first a bit like the fixies of today—endearing to a select group willing to work around their idiosyncrasies.

Women were initially hampered from biking on Ordinaries just as they had been hampered from riding velocipedes– by heavy skirts as well as Victorian ideals of maternal and female behavior. Yet more women flaunted these rules than one might initially suspect. Circus performers were amongst the first to have access to practice on the hard-to-mount machines. Soon, though, irrepressibly athletic women like Canadian Louise Armaindo and Elsa von Blumen from the U.S. carved out careers for themselves and a path forward for women to ride the high wheel.

They suffered ridicule yet also gained respect for doing so.

Elsa and Louise Go High Wheel

One of the first indications that women might be able to excel at riding and racing the high-wheel bicycle appeared in Western newspapers in the fall of 1879. A seamstress named Lizzie Baymer competed against two other women, an Addie Lee and a Mrs. Martin, in a two-hour race that was repeated for four consecutive nights as an entertaining interlude to a men's race. Dressed in a black velvet outfit that included "trunks" and flesh-colored tights, Lizzie won all the contests.

At the point that she began biking, Lizzie Baymer had participated in at least one other endurance sport–

pedestrianism. All the rage in the 1860s, pedestrianism was a grueling test of staying power, requiring participants to walk dozens of miles in contests that lasted up to six days and included little rest or sleep. Despite how boring walking competitions might sound to us now, these races drew huge crowds. After a few years, women demonstrated their endurance at these money-making pedestrian spectacles, though more conservative newspapers frowned both at the exhibitions and at the contests' possible effects on female health.

Pedestrianism was a training ground for the launch of bicycle racing as the high-wheel gained adherents. The first bicycle race in the U.S. was purported to take place in Boston in 1878. By 1879, Lizzie Baymer and a handful of other women had procured machines and learned to ride, possibly at Fred Merrill's bicycle school in San Francisco. After just a few appearances on the bicycle, though, Lizzie disappeared from the press.

Meanwhile on the east coast, a young woman named Elsa von Blumen was making headlines. Like Lizzie Baymer, Elsa got her start in pedestrianism, and in 1880 she purchased a high wheel from Pope Manufacturing. Elsa von Blumen's real name was Caroline Wilhelmina Kiner, and she was born in 1862 in Florida, though soon after her birth moved with her family to Rochester, New York.

Elsa likely adopted the stage name von Blumen in homage to another female pedestrian—they were called "pedestriennes" in the press—named Bertha von Hillern, who had emigrated to the U.S. from Germany in 1877 and made a big splash as a strong, fast walker. Elsa's manager was a man who coached a number of female walkers. He called himself Burt Miller, though his real name was William Roosevelt.

With Burt Miller by her side, Elsa undertook exhibitions of her bicycle riding, eventually beginning to race against horses on outdoor tracks. These races generally gave her a lap or two handicap, and she consistently won, taking prize money upwards of $200 and the admiration of crowds in the thousands. Early on, Elsa fashioned a demure bicycle costume that she stuck to almost exclusively through years of riding and racing. It consisted of a short, tailored gray jacket over a blouse, a short fringed gray skirt, grey knickers, dark stockings, and dark boots. Her hat was of the same gray, jaunty and with a poof of feathers on top.

In addition to her modest outfit, in all of her communications Elsa tried to convey propriety and respectability. She denounced gambling at her races and promoted biking as a healthful activity for women.

In contrast, Elsa's main competitor Louise Armaindo took a more brash, aggressive approach. Born Louise Brisbois in 1857 in a farm town called St. Anne (now part of the Montreal metro area), Louise left home as a teen and tried various athletic endeavors–trapeze artist, body builder, race walker–in order to make her way in the world. Louise became a professional cyclist at about the age of 23, though in newspaper accounts she claimed she was 20.

Her age was a moving marker all her life and she never worried about lying to the press. It was only through the joint research work of myself and author Ann M. Hall that Louise's birth and death dates were more firmly established through parish records and U.S. Census data.

Shifting to bike racing in 1881 from pedestrianism seemed a smart move on Louise's part. She had the stamina needed to outride many men and all the women she first encountered. As Elsa was on the East Coast and she lived in Chicago, Louise could also exploit, for a short time, the local novelty of a woman cycling on the high-wheel or Ordinary.

Within a year of learning to bike in the late fall of 1881, Louise Armaindo showed some of the toughest male racers that she could beat them at tests of endurance. She wasn't shy about demanding a handicap and always tried to play it both ways—flaunting her prowess as the "best" woman rider while pressing for maximum advantage because she was female. In March of 1882 she took to a track in St. Louis, aiming to do a six-day, 600-mile ride. At the end of six days of endurance riding—at least one hundred miles per day—she had gone 617.5 miles, spending just 20 hours off the track in total for sleeping. Louise and her manager Tom Eck, both immigrants from Canada looking for their main chance, claimed this to be the longest bicycle ride on record for anyone, male or female.

Louise and other early racing cyclists and their managers seemed to count on the fact that the size of the country and the newness and spectacle of the sport meant they could make claims that might turn out eventually to be... not entirely accurate. Best practices of laying a precise track and having objective scorers weren't always heeded in the headlong rush to race.

It turned out Louise's erstwhile rival Elsa von Blumen had already attempted a 1,000-mile ride earlier, in January-February 1882, that was more grueling than what Louise managed in St. Louis. It was first reported that Elsa successfully finished the 1,000-mile ride, but as accounts eked out in the press, it began to circulate that her "official" mile scorer was actually Burt's brother-in-law. This irregularity was looked on askance by the bicycling press, especially on the East Coast where the newly formed League of American Wheelmen (LAW) was trying to organize bicycling as a dignified endeavor and sport.

Eventually the League would turn on Elsa, Louise, and the whole idea of women riding high wheels. But before that happened, the two women competed against each other. In July of 1882, over six days they did 30 two-mile heats; Louise won 21. The following month, she teamed up with Elsa at a freshly-built racetrack on the grounds of Coney Island's Sea Beach Palace Hotel. Together they raced against a young newcomer, William J. Morgan. For this single race Louise and Elsa functioned as a team, though they were known to be rivals.

The press reports considered Louise to be the most graceful rider of the three. She also showed herself to be faster and fiercer than Elsa. In a race that lasted six days, a common format in that time, the two women partners started strong, gaining an eight-mile lead over William Morgan's first day solo performance. By the middle of the race, though, a hungry Louise gorged on cucumber pickles during her rest period. Back on the wheel and careening around the track she took a painful header over the top of the handlebars. The pair lost their considerable advantage over William Morgan and ended up covering 465 miles together to his 467 miles. Yet even after those sapping six days of racing, Louise challenged Elsa to a 50-mile race the very next day and beat her handily.

Some months later, Louise got her chance to vanquish William Morgan in a different six-day event. May of 1883 delivered one of the sweetest victories in her approximately eight-year career. The press giddily reported that riding against William Morgan and another new racer, William Woodside, over the course of six days Louise Armaindo managed to hold her own then take the lead, setting a new world's endurance cycling record. She earned the title "Queen of the Wheel" from the St. Paul, Minnesota *Daily Globe*[14].

As a brash and seemingly fearless rider, Louise wowed crowds as effectively as any present-day Olympian. Partially through her outspoken personality—when she talked to the press she tended to boast—and partially encouraged by her handlers, Louise "the wonder woman racer" drew attention. She was also an outlier and an individualist, breaking all the Victorian codes due to her outfits and what was considered immodest speech. Many men were drawn to the salacious spectacle of seeing her scantily dressed while riding, though her audiences included plenty of women fans, too. After her early wins and attention, Louise veered toward ever-flashier outfits with sequins and lace, while Elsa clung to the same ensemble every contest. One paper called a race Louise was cycling in noteworthy only for her scanty attire.

When it came to performance, Louise delivered. Still, Victorian newspapers sometimes hardly knew whether to cheer or chide her efforts. There may also have been an undercurrent of racism in the coverage she received, as Louise was olive-skinned and had some Métis (Canadian Indigenous) heritage. Her riding was so strong and her endurance so great, however, that the press found it hard to ignore her. Elsa was never able to vanquish her in direct competition and eventually refused to race Louise, leaving Louise alone in her willingness to go up against first-class male riders.

Races were also profitable. Through the 1880s and 1890s from a few pennies to a half-dollar could be charged daily for entry to a six-day race. This format of racing a few hours a day for six days had been used for pedestrian contests. It built audience excitement, and also got around a rule that made racing on Sundays unlawful. Though race venues were often smoky, poorly heated and ventilated, and very uncomfortable for the athletes, they were centrally located (like the old Madison Square Gardens) and fierce competition caused anticipation to build day-to-day until big crowds massed for the sixth day's finale.

Between 1883 and 1888, Louise traveled incessantly to whatever cities would help her put together races. She challenged both male and female riders. Unsanctioned by the LAW, which had become the authority on bicycle racing in the United States, these endurance tests pitted Louise against anyone willing to match the wagers she or her manager Tom (T.W.) Eck posted at local newspaper offices.

In an illustration from an 1885 *Springfield Wheelmen's Gazette*, Louise rested her hand on her hip as she gazed straight toward the viewer. In this depiction she chose a fancy, one-piece saque, which was a long, but barely bum-covering jacket whose lace flounces didn't hide her powerful thighs. A tight-fitting cycling cap, short-cropped curls, and a big medal pinned prominently to her chest all added to the picture of self-assurance she radiated.

While beating Elsa von Blumen the few times they raced each other may have been good for Louise's ego, there weren't enough other women racers to hone her skills against. This started to shift nearer the end of the decade, as a crop of strong athletic women were drawn to the sport. Mostly from working and middle-class backgrounds, these women got little support from the League or the bicycle press. As we will see, the newness of the sport and of the idea of women racing made them vulnerable to financial exploitation by their male managers.

Patriarchal domination in the form of the League of American Wheelman began to work toward the end of the 1880s to—first through editorial commentary, later through blacklisting venues that hosted women's races—make it seem that women racing bicycles was vulgar. The League's main goal was exerting control over an exuberant pastime that quickly became a sport. However, the "gentlemen" who initially could afford bicycling favored amateur racing—pure tests of athletic skill with lots of back slapping and perhaps a medal at the end. Individuals in the working or middle classes like Louise wanted to use their strength and stamina to get ahead: to get paid as professionals.

Louise was willing to accept the hardships and the occasional jackpots. But in the 1880s society wasn't ready for women to play hard, wear unconventional outfits (leggings and long pants) and win over men. Even so, a new era of racing was just over the horizon, and with it, a re-think about what constituted a bicycling "costume."

Tricyclist Belva

L ouise entered high-wheel bicycling at its absolute heyday. Young men of medium means all clamored to purchase a wheel, join their local bicycle club, and head out on weekend or even weekday tours. The bicycle clubs were social venues, and through them ran a vein of camaraderie and kinship that was bolstered by a militaristic penchant for fancy uniforms, special signals and formations, rules and regulations, and of course, a tendency to exclude women.

In most cases it was an (almost) unconscious paternalism. Women were considered delicate and in need of caretaking, and of course many women reinforced this stereotype by default because there were few means for independence. It was a common chicken vs. egg conundrum. Women became "consumptive" and weak from too much time indoors. Those of lesser means got strong through exceedingly hard kitchen and household labor but had little to no time for rest or restorative exercise. It was also difficult and dangerous to ride a bike when hampered by ground-dragging wool skirts and pounds of figure-cinching underwear. The culture crimped womens' style and, at the same time, conditioned them to think they were too weak to be able to enjoy bicycling or other exertion.

There was one factor exerting a bit of counterpressure: cultural courtship rituals. Bikes were democratizing, expensive relative to many mens' incomes yet requiring little maintenance and upkeep. For a larger cross-section of the population they fostered mobility and the freedom to roam. Once these men started roaming, they realized how pleasant it was, on a lovely spring afternoon, to get away from the density and dirt of cities. And their next thought? How pleasant it would be to have a sweetheart along for the ride.

Bicycle designers realized this appeal, and spent time creating a machine that was accessible to riders that weren't as nimble as the average 20-year-old male. The early result of these efforts was the tricycle. As he had with the high-wheel, British inventor James Starley played a starring role in popularizing the tricycle. In 1876, he developed the Coventry Lever Tricycle and a year later the Coventry Rotary. These two machines, though heavy and cumbersome, started a tricycling trend. By 1877, Coventry's release of the Salvo tricycle had critics calling it Starley's masterwork. The Salvo had two huge wheels that sandwiched the rider in between them, and a tiny guide wheel in front. Queen Victoria bought two.

By 1880 these models were available in the U.S. For members of different bicycle clubs, the tricycle was the perfect way to get young women involved, though not *too* involved, because tricycles were slow and unwieldy alongside the Ordinary, and they needed so much more space for storage. Still, they were the ultimate gentleman's or gentlewoman's machine. On mild weekends, prosperous young men could wheel out for a leisure ride with their sisters and girlfriends, away from the chiding of older female chaperones. Some of these girls and women formed their own tricycle clubs, and sometimes they even reportedly went bike touring on their own, without the sheltering presence of the men.

Belva Ann Lockwood didn't have the time or temperament for social tricycling. Belva was one of the first female lawyers in the United States. She had to petition Ulysses S. Grant to be allowed to practice, and by 1879 she petitioned the U.S. Supreme Court to be able to bring cases before them. Newspapers reported Belva riding a tricycle around the recently paved "asphaltum" streets of Washington DC. At first they labeled her an "independent girl," though by the time she bought her tricycle she was a married mother and an established attorney.

Belva used her tricycle for mobility during working hours—visiting clients and delivering documents. Once the press caught on to her daily use of the tricycle, she was mercilessly denigrated. One reporter described Belva's cycling as "ludicrous gyrations." She was ridiculed for red stockings that showed her ankles "with each turn of the wheel." Yet that same reporter chided Lockwood for her "appearance on the Washington avenues in a coal scuttle bonnet of the last century."[15] The papers even claimed her looks scared other women away from tricycling. She couldn't win—she was too daring and too old-fashioned simultaneously.

As soon as she ran for President in 1884, the first of two campaigns, the vitriol increased. Her stockings and her hair came under constant scrutiny. The fact that she was a tricycle rider was deemed ridiculous. In spite of all the critique (and though of course no other women could vote for her as they didn't have the right to vote yet) she managed to rack up 4,000 votes in the 1884 election.

Belva was a self-proclaimed suffragist. She worked for women's rights, continuing to ride her tricycle around town to see clients and do errands. When her first trike was run over by a carriage in front of the White House, she got another. She was considered the only woman tricyclist seen regularly on Washington's streets for a number of years. By the late 1880s, however, a group of almost 300 local women had organized a tricycling club. This led papers to speculate that there were more than 1,000 female tricyclists in total in the region.

Gaslighting prospective women riders by claiming that riders like Belva were so scandalous or immoral that they prohibited "decent" women from taking to the wheel wasn't uncommon. It was part of the patriarchal mindset. An opinion writer for the *Wheelmen's Gazette* speculated in 1889 that it was Louise Armaindo's fault that women didn't switch from the tricycle to the just-released safety cycles. The writer believed the notoriety of racing women and the upsurge in races had an "uncleanly" effect upon the sport. The racers' short breeches–under skirts–were the greatest affront, the writer noted. He didn't condemn women outright for racing, as long as they "veil[ed] their bicycular [sic] motions by some manner of modest and womanly dress."[16]

This same argument—that brazen women kept (or should keep) respectable women from biking—would be recycled on the West Coast later in the 1890s when a hack journalist interviewed the local bike merchant who alleged prostitutes in Portland rode their bikes in full fancy costumes and scared supposedly decent women away from riding.

Due to this type of censure or not, Belva Lockwood always stuck to sober dresses on her tricycle. Once her red-stocking articles made the news, she even had a special dashboard installed on her tricycle so no one could view her legs if her skirts flapped upward while she pedaled. Throughout her lifetime she openly objected to the idea of what she called "chaperonage": the notion that women needed constant oversight by a male relative. She continued to argue that boys and girls should be educated with an "equal sense of responsibility." Belva died in 1917, three years short of women receiving the right to vote in the United States.

The Adventurers

In bicycling's early eras, the best place for women to truly enjoy the feeling of freedom the bicycle bestowed was out on the open road, bicycle touring. Elizabeth Robins, a native of Philadelphia, came to understand this. She married artist Joseph Pennell in 1884 and immediately departed for an epic cycling journey from London to Canterbury on a pedal-powered tandem tricycle. Elizabeth was an art and food critic and enjoyed many fruitful book collaborations with her artist husband, including five books based on their tricycle and later bicycle tours in England, Italy, France, and the Alps.

Elizabeth also believed she was the first woman to try to cross the Alps by bicycle in 1898. Her bicycle was a Rover safety, a fixie-style bike (no freewheel mechanism) with a pneumatic brake that required pumping up before steep descents. In other words, she either pedaled or took her feet off the pedals and put them on a peg rest to coast, then pumped the brakes as needed.

She fortified herself for these alpine climbs with double breakfasts—together she and Joseph could make more than 100 miles a day. Though she had twenty years of cycling experience, the twisty mountain roads were without safety guard rails and the 1,000 foot drops were harrowing. She described the ascents and descents superbly, but it's a pity that as a food critic she didn't give more ink to what she ate, and how she felt through it all. How did she keep her hat on in chilly mountain winds? What did she do when she got her period? Was there shammy butter back then? Alas, none of these intriguing questions get answers, though her book *Over the Alps on a Bicycle* is a fun and engaging account that encourages touring: "I wanted to see if I could cross the Alps on a bicycle. I did—and any woman who rides—and knows how to ride—a good strong machine fitted with a good strong brake on each wheel, who will be wise enough not to let it get away with her... nor to play herself out by riding it on a long steep ascent, and who is not afraid of work, may learn what pleasure there is in the exploit."[17]

Elizabeth's book was also one of the first bike touring guide books—well-written and with some good advice for the cyclist of 1885. Her travel-writing contemporary Fanny Bullock Workman married Dr. Willam Workman in 1881. Unlike the Pennells, whose work helped fund their trips, the Workmans had plenty of money and traveled constantly, sometimes with an entourage, sometimes on bicycle. Their trips were monumental: a 2,000 mile trek around Spain; 14,000 miles exploring the Indian subcontinent.

Elizabeth's books were more literary—written with the reader in mind—yet also more self-absorbed, while Fanny was intent on thorough travel reporting. Fanny provided geographical and historical backgrounds on places they visited, and also did a great job telling some of the strange meals they encountered along the way. Both Fanny and Elizabeth hewed to Victorian ideals and eschewed bloomers, tights, and pants as their regular riding costumes, though there is a memorable photo of Bullock Workman in a knickerbocker-and-puttees ensemble. How these two awesome travelers kept themselves and their voluminous garments clean and dealt with things like menstruation would make for fascinating reading, but they never told.

CHAPTER THREE

Off to the Races (1889-1894)

New Blood, New Wheels

1889 was a tricky year of transition for women's racing and also for bicycles in general. Men's racing was in upheaval as the newly-formed American Cyclists Union struggled and failed to wrest control of racing from the League of American Wheelmen. The conflict led to fewer men's races. Though Louise and Elsa had been nearly the only racing women through most of the 1880s, by 1888 the new crop of young female athletes had emerged at the exact moment that the Ordinary was making its last laps as the racing machine of choice. The so-called safety bicycle was on the horizon—John Starley had formed a new firm and introduced a commercial successful model called the Rover in 1885 in England, and in the United States more and more bicycle dealers were stocking this type of bike. With two wheels of equal size and pneumatic tires, the safety would be a safer and more comfortable ride than the Ordinary, and riders started to buy the new models over the last few years of the decade.

But racers and race promoters who had bet on the Ordinary were reluctant. And women's racing on the Ordinary was attracting new attention. An exciting six-day women's race in Pittsburgh in November, 1888 brought thousands of spectators to see if a local girl named Lottie Stanley could take the decisive lead over eight other female contestants. All nine of the women were new to high-wheel bicycle racing but had trained together with local race promoter William B. Troy. Lottie vanquished her competition, and subsequently a 100-mile race was scheduled for a little later during Christmas week. Right after the Pittsburgh race, though, an unproven claim surfaced that the race promoter had tried to fix the race for another racer, Helen Baldwin. Further reports had promoter Troy absconding with the gate receipts. When the Pittsburgh track was officially surveyed and found to be shorter than advertised, racers' mile totals were revised. These improprieties didn't help the cause of female racing.

Yet once Lottie won the Christmas race and another in Pittsburgh, New York City race organizers tried to cash in on the sudden popularity of women's races by scheduling a February contest at the old Madison Square Garden. Louise Armaindo and Elsa von Blumen, by now each over 30 years old, were both determined to show their skills. By early February, a group of women including Louise and Elsa decamped to the city for training.

Women's racing had already been thoroughly criticized by the League of American Wheelmen, and many commentators described the young athletic women who wanted to ride and race as unseemly. While newspaper and magazine writers admitted the women showed pluck riding skittish bicycles with front wheels of 50 inches or more in circumference, their objections were three-fold: racing was physically dangerous; it damaged female "sensibilities;" and finally, they claimed without proof that it hurt the overall reputation of bicycling.

The contests were also very popular. At six day races, women generally rode eight hours per day—two four-hour segments with a rest in between. In spite of this demonstration of their athletic stamina and ability, papers referred to these women bicyclists as a "bevy" of girls, calling them "fair" and describing their outfits in considerable detail. They wore "woolen leggings of various color and design, with tight-fitting jackets and knit skull-caps" one newspaper reported, displaying to advantage their shapely figures."[18] As usual, the newspaper audience was assumed to be as interested in the amount of skin the riders showed as in their skill and brawn.

The February 1889 race between fourteen women riders proved to be intense. There were injuries when women collided with bystanders wandering on to the track. Early on Louise Armaindo was the clear crowd and press favorite—the newspapers gave her kudos for supreme staying power and mentioned her previous wins over male competitors. Pittsburgh native Lottie Stanley was described as strong and incredibly determined.

"Clad in her bright blue satin jacket, trimmed with ermine, a blue jacket cap with a feather fastened rakishly to the crown, and feet encased in blue canvas shoes, she sets the pace for others, spurting now and then, and gaining a lap at her pleasure."[19]

It was Louise's chance for a real comeback. In January with a 10-mile handicap she beat two male competitors in Lincoln, Nebraska to the applause of an admiring crowd. But by the February six-day race, she wasn't up to the grind. She appeared on the track for short bursts, and some papers reported that she was continually "worried" off the track by Lottie Stanley and other racers ganging up and forcing her to the sidelines. Whatever jostling might have happened on the track, Louise only had the lead for the first few hours of racing, and after that she dropped further and further behind. Elsa Von Blumen—in the same dove gray pant-and-skirt outfit she'd always worn—tried valiantly to keep up with and attempted to wrestle the lead from Lottie Stanely, but to no avail. From the group of the dozen racing women, Lottie in her blue canvas shoes emerged victorious. She took a victory lap to an absolute crescendo of cheers and applause.

Yet as the spectators filed out of the Garden, another type of ruckus began. The newspapers quickly reported that Lottie claimed the race organizers owed her $500 for her first-place win. This was an echo of her grumbling about being shorted by the race promoter after her victorious 1888 race in Pittsburgh. In the next day's reporting it was revealed that of the prize money the top three winners were supposed to receive a share of, they didn't get a penny. Also revealed was an inequitable system that had racing women on salary with their managers for $25 per week when they were racing, $10 a week when they were not. Lottie admitted to the newspapers that this was accurate but said that she was promised a $500 bonus if she took top honors. Eventually, though the managers grumbled about the economics of the race, they paid Lottie $250. The entire sordid tussle dumped more bad press on women's racing.

Tricky Annie

S ome of the early racers like Louise Armaindo were seasoned veterans of the circus, where riding first the velocipede and then the Ordinary was not an unusual feat. Rider Annie Sylvester based her entire career on what was called "trick," "fancy," or circus-style riding. Circus riders were allowed, even expected to wear revealing and bright outfits, and the ability to move back and forth between the circus and other performance gigs was key to building up the talent pool of female riders and racers that formed in the late 1880s into the 1890s.

Annie Elizabeth James was born around 1866 in the tiny town of Florissant, Missouri, now a suburb of St. Louis. Like Louise, she never gave her exact age in news reports. Both Annie and Louise seemed to grasp the rules of the emerging youth culture—be forever young and forever pretty—to appease the culture's age-old desire for women to somehow simultaneously fill the roles of lady in public and wanton woman in the bedroom. She took the stage name Sylvester, and found a steady career not in acting, her first choice, but in bicycle trick riding. She also drove chariots in the circus and could handle horses and wheels. While Louise's popularity rose and fell sharply over her career span, Annie managed for most of her career to receive a steady stream of positive press. It was hinted she should race against Louise in the early years of their time in the news spotlight.

But after a bicycle race or two, none reported with Louise Armaindo, Annie stuck to tricks. By 1885 she had a series of gigs at skating rinks, showing her skill maneuvering the Ordinary. Women typically were charged a quarter to rent roller skates and see Annie's show. Gents were required to pay an extra quarter to get a glimpse of Annie on her bike.

Annie's routine was somewhat similar to Carrie Moore's, until she or one of her managers conceived of the idea of removing both the curved frame and the small attached back wheel from one of her high-wheeled bicycles. Voila! This left a direct-drive big wheel, pedals and saddle, and a straight set of handlebars attached by a front fork.

Some people labeled it a monocycle. Annie mastered the apparatus and later made claim to be the world's first unicyclist. She was likely not the first but was one of the first women to publicly perform the skill. Her tricks included perching atop a 12-foot-high pyramid of wicker tables balancing her wheel. As *The Wheel* noted in 1885, "Annie Sylvester, bicyclienne, is delighting the natives of the "wild" northwest by her graceful exhibitions."[20]

There's that word—graceful. It's the dog whistle that means the press approved. Annie's costumes were no less scanty than Louise's–bright tights, form-fitting bodysuit, artful drapes and bric-a-brac. Yet somehow Annie got a pass, and was always referred to as a lady. Perhaps Louise's olive complexion as well as her boasting played a part in her not-as-favorable press.

While Annie's working bicycle career provided steady income, her personal life was a continual drama. Her third marriage was not the charm—she shot her third husband Louis Holladay to death after he reportedly tried to kill her in a drunken rage. Holladay's family was wealthy, and his death in 1899 (along with the subsequent trial publicity) put Annie's life into chaos. She pleaded self-defense and was eventually let off. But the torrent of publicity began to tilt more negative, and more importantly, Annie was out of work. She ended her days in poverty in a tiny seaside cottage in Redondo Beach, California, dying there in 1938.

Safety First

By 1890, the Ordinary's decade-long run as the bicycle of choice was truly over. The middle-class men of the early 1880s who formed the cycling clubs, bought the fancy uniforms, practiced the drills and formations and went on long weekend rides were now considered old men. The small groups of young women who took to the tricycle were now in the midst of family life and motherhood.

Once the racing season of 1889-1890 sputtered out, the new generation of younger women that experimented on the Ordinary were faced with a shift to newfangled safety bicycles. Louise Armaindo unfortunately did not make the transition. In the winter of 1889-1890 she took a trip with a small group of women Ordinary riders to England and raced a few races but never got first place. Back in the U.S. she struggled to make a living, turned to pedestrianism and walking races for income for a short period and continued to throw out challenges in newspapers trying to find competitors for 50 or 100-mile races. By 1895 she washed up in Buffalo, New York, back in the newspapers after she jumped from her burning rooming house building, smashed her legs to bits, and sued the rooming house owners. The suit dragged on, and eventually Louise was the loser. She died crippled and in obscurity in Montreal in 1900.

Women's races had continued at a fast pace through 1889-1890, and other racers besides Lottie Stanley showed promise. But by 1890 everyone's eyes turned to the beautiful new safety cycles. In Britain the Rover—introduced in 1895—was considered a blockbuster success that put cycling onto the city streets. Its two wheels of nearly equal dimensions, rear-wheel drive via a chain, and pneumatic tires were technological advances that translated into popular success.

To most riders of the Ordinary, the new safety looked like a more enjoyable way to bike. It was faster and easier to maneuver up hills. With a price tag in England of an affordable twenty pounds, the Rover was advertised as "faster than a bicycle and safer than a tricycle" by its manufacturers Starley & Sutton. This vein of marketing was an interesting twist, implying that the tricycle was unsafe. The estimate was that 500-1000 women in the U.S. capital city rode tricycles because of the perceived idea that they were the safe, womanly way to cycle. Now the tide of social mores (and the accompanying expected wardrobe) was shifting again.

The Rover came to U.S. shores in 1887, and by the spring of 1888, a bicycle dealer predicted women would love the new safeties: "This spring and summer... the fair ones will take to the bicycle... the novelty of the thing will be so far gone no lady will hesitate to ride for fear of attracting too much notice to herself." The same dealer suggested that women should have riding habits made similar to those for horsewomen, though he didn't go so far as suggest pants. He did say biking women "should not be tied or strapped up to such an extent as to prevent the utmost freedom of the use of every muscle."[21]

By 1890, the Rover and other safety models like it were displacing the Ordinary. As Luther Porter put it in his book *Wheels and Wheeling*: "[The safety's] suitability for all ages, conditions, and sexes together with the ease with which it could be mastered soon made it immensely popular."[22] Concurrently, city cycling was boosted by new laws treating bicycles as vehicles (in New York in 1887), as well as the marked improvements to roads via the use of macadam.

It helped that the consumer/mass market age was dawning. Up to this time, many new innovative bicycle designs were, no surprise, adopted by the well-to-do first. They could afford to snap up the latest trinket. They rode in parks and along paths and found biking a great way to display their trendiness and their prowess on the wheel, as well as flaunt the latest fashions. Famed businessman, financier and philanthropist "Diamond" Jim Brady bought his mistress Lillian Russell a gem-encrusted bicycle straight from Tiffany's display window.

Fairly quickly, the increased supply of safety models in the U.S. also dropped bike prices, which allowed bicycling to trickle down to all segments of society. Riding a bike became an achievable freedom for the working and middle classes—no need for barn or horse food, carriage, or cash for cabs. That cycling became a universal mania in the early 1890s is reflected in several tunes of the decade with the word "cyclist" or "bicycle" in them, and the many periodicals covering cycling as a social sport, hobby, and a means of local, personal transportation. There were at least a dozen bicycle novels from the period. New bicycle customs sprang up, such as the bicycle chaperone (imagine how popular they were!) and the bicycle wedding or elopement. With better roads, cyclists could more easily get around and even leave their cities for excursions into the countryside.

Darting Toward a Drop Frame

But before women would begin buying the new bikes in massive numbers, one additional technological improvement was needed. It was implemented by designer W.E. Smith. The story is that Smith purchased a safety and as soon as his wife saw the new bicycle she wanted to ride it. It was still difficult, however, for any woman wearing a skirt to get a leg up over the top bar of the frame. So Smith removed it, found an investment partner in 1887, and the drop-frame bicycle was born. In vol. 59 of *Iron Age* magazine, writer E.D. Sewell said Mrs. Smith rode the company's new bike, named the Dart, in a demonstration down Pennsylvania Avenue in early 1888, making her the first woman to publicly bike on the new drop frame in the U.S.[23] By 1892, bike manufacturer and Union Army colonel Albert Augustus Pope also introduced a drop-frame ladies' model, and many others followed. There was one drawback: a diamond-frame bike was steadier, and more stable.

Yet now the womens' cycling revolution could begin in earnest. This isn't to say that cultural approval was instant. In fact there was a flurry of contradictory messaging to women who wanted to bicycle. Some doctors decried the overexertion the bicycle was said to foster, though most medical professionals agreed that women needed more outdoor exercise. Bikes were accused of deflowering younger women, causing spontaneous orgasms, encouraging loose behavior, and rendering women unfit for childbearing. The confusion and objections to women bicyclists as unfeminine and immodest was the result of entrenched Victorian attitudes, both from men and women. Social conservatives started their attacks back in the days of the velocipede, and they never truly let up. Skirts—how short they were, how much ankle they allowed to peek out, how unsuitably they clung to lady bicyclists' figures, and how women were expected to keep their corsets on while riding and maintain their hourglass silhouettes—filled pages of magazines.

In spite of mixed messaging, over the next few years thousands of women across the United States would begin to feel the joy of hopping in the saddle and pedaling on down the road.

Frances, the Bicycling Suffragist

Frances E. Willard was a late-in-life bicyclist who illuminated all the different cultural influences regarding bicycling. Willard was an academic, an ardent teetotaler and a firm believer in women's right to vote.

Always called Frank by her mother, in her writings she admitted she was a wild child until the age of 16, when she was forced into long skirts and found familial duties to be her new and not entirely welcome lot. She was deeply religious, bookish, and hardworking. Willard's first job was as a teacher, and in short order she became president of the Evanston College of Ladies and Dean of the Women's College when Evanston merged with

Northwestern. By that time Willard was turning towards her second career—constant critic of alcohol's effects, and a temperance reformer. She was elected president of the Women's Christian Temperance Union (WCTU) in 1879 and held that position her entire life.

Willard helped create and mold the WCTU and argued passionately for alcohol prohibition and female suffrage. She had been one of the thousands of American women able for the first time to get a college education, and she had a great affinity for this peer group. After she became powerful in the WCTU, she continued to nurture this connection to the women of her generation. She was interested in being a person of moral strength and strived toward that ideal, as well as revering a concept of home life and domesticity that included a broad notion of what a family should consist of, i.e. a place where one received welcome, affection, care, and respect. Identified by some historians as a lesbian, Willard had a series of deep alliances and strong long term relationships with women.

Colonel Pope had given her a tricycle in 1886. But it was after the death of her mother and an illness akin to a nervous breakdown in 1893 that Willard took up the bicycle in earnest. By then she was past 50—an age where women were considered crones. And she herself commented on the fact that she believed she was an old woman learning to bike.

She also believed biking was a wondrous social invention, key to keeping young men from the evils of alcohol and bringing more strength to the institution of the family. She practiced the tricycle in her Evanston hometown in the "80s. However, to her, the safety bicycle was an entirely different undertaking than a trike. She thought the deck was stacked against her in wanting to learn: "At 53, I was at more disadvantage than most people, for not only had I the impedimenta that results from the unnatural style of dress, but I also suffered from the sedentary habits of a lifetime. And that small world of those who loved me best... did not encourage me, but thought I should break my bones and "spoil my future."[24]

Willard was aware that other bicycling women were looked at askance in the 1880s—she saw Bertha von Hillern, a young German pedestrian who also gave exhibitions of her riding skill, and noted that von Hillern subsequently was made out to be "some sort of semi-monster... a traitor to the feminine guild."[26] She realized lack of balance and her fears around falling were her biggest hurdles. Her companion Lady Henry Somerset gave her a safety bicycle that she christened "Gladys" and she learned to ride it, though she freely admitted it took her three months, many lessons, and lots of sympathetic helpers willing to run alongside her bike through numerous sessions while she gained confidence and a sense of balance.

Willard learned to ride the safety for her own wellbeing, but in photos she never looked comfortable or joyful. She persevered because of a conviction that there were many more women enervated by the work of life who needed to also experience the health-giving joys of bicycling. As befits a dedicated social reformer, she proselytized what she learned by writing a short book, *A Wheel Within a Wheel: How I Learned to Ride the Bicycle, With Some Reflections by the Way*.

In a photo included in the book and captioned "At Last," Willard was shown successfully riding Gladys. She actually looked grittily determined rather than happy, swathed in the "unnatural" outfit of a long, double-breasted navy blue jacket, heavy ankle-length skirt, straw hat and black "bicycle" boots. Perhaps it was the strain of trying to reconcile the freedom of biking with the strict ideal of a woman's role as sober regulator of family stability. Or maybe her boots were too tight.

Willard saw the bicycle as support for a moral life. She thought deeply about women's rights, but her perspective was limited by her time, and her privileged and fairly prosperous upper-middle-class upbringing. Her conception couldn't (yet) include a more relaxed approach to her own sexuality and love for other women. She was debated by Ida B. Wells at one point, who accused Willard of using racist language and promoting the idea of the danger of "black mobs" in her defense of temperance.

But her achievement with bicycle riding was, she said, "exceedingly" satisfying, and riding a bicycle was her metaphor for success in life. She died in 1898, just five years after she learned to ride.

Wrecked (by Anonymous)

A girl, a wheel,

A shock, a squeal,

A header, a thump,

A girl in a lump,

A bloomer all torn,

A maiden forlorn.

(From *Bicycle People* by Roland C. Geist, 1978, Acropolis Books)

CHAPTER FOUR

Irrational Dress

(1894-1899)

An Outfit History

Much has been written about what women wore while biking during that first big bike boom. Accepted wisdom was that the bicycle brought bloomers—a.k.a. women's first pants—into fashion. It is true that Amelia Bloomer was an advocate for women's right to vote and other freedoms. It was also true that Bloomer specifically promoted a change in dress standards in her writings, especially in the women-led periodical she edited called *The Lily*.

Born in 1818, Amelia married in 1840 and got her chops as a journalist from working on her husband Dexter's newspaper. She was made editor of *The Lily* in 1849, and was a believer in women's rights. When in 1851 she spotted acquaintance and fellow women's rights activist Elizabeth Smith Miller wearing loose blousy pants topped with a shorter-than-normal dress, she adopted the outfit, and just happened to be seen by a journalist while wearing it.

Bloomer was already known as an author and journalist and had a catchy surname to boot. Thus the press pounced, naming her dress-and-pants combo the Bloomer Costume. She didn't invent it nor was she the first to wear it. Additionally, it caused far more uproar in the newspapers than its initial influence on women's fashion warranted. Bloomer stopped wearing bloomers in 1859, years before the velocipede swept in. By 1869, the height of the velocipede's influence, Bloomer was wearing conventional skirts with crinolines. Bloomer herself, as far as the record shows, never put a foot to the pedal of a velocipede, Ordinary, or safety bicycle, and died in 1894.

That's fascinating, as it is exactly the year the bloomer became a real influence in the slow-building movement for reform in women's dress. Though it was truly slow. There was a group of women (and a few men) that continued to talk about womens' burden of heavy, dirt-skimming skirts, many pounds of underwear, and innards-squeezing corsets. These reformers were at the core of what is called the "rational dress" movement. But while the movement wanted women to be able to don practical outfits that were also comfortable, it didn't eschew outright the skirt or the corset.

Amazingly, a review of illustrations from the late 1860s and 1870s, as well as the few surviving photos of women riding and racing on the high-wheeled Ordinary, shows that in spite of the need to have freedom of movement, most of them continued with corsets. Corsets put pressure on a woman's entire breathing apparatus and internal organs and squelched the ability to take a deep expansive breath. But fashion of the 19th and early 20th century continued to dictate that a woman should have a 20-inch waist (or smaller). For the most part women complied to the standard, or tried to. Corsets were also a class issue—field-working women and the very poor couldn't afford them. One difficulty in letting go of a corset was that once a waist was constricted day after day, the torso wanted the support of that ongoing binding—corset wearers grew accustomed not only to how they looked under dresses but also how they felt. "Night wear" corsets were common, and only slightly less restrictive than the daytime model.

You can see in photos that professional velocipede riders like Carrie Moore tried to design costumes that had the best of both worlds—they had snug, fitted waists for appearance, and retained a skirt, but also included leggings or some kind of "trunks" underneath the skirt, with stockings and boots completing the ensemble. Once the Ordinary came on the scene, the difficulty of wearing a skirt increased, because a rider was perched directly above the large bespoked front wheel, instead of between two wheels of more or less equal size. The chance of getting a skirt or petticoat caught up was intensified.

So what were women to do? The skirt, and society's insistence that women wear one, definitely held back the popularity of the Ordinary. From only looking at the illustrations and photos, it seemed that 1870s women who wanted to stay on the side of propriety had to keep their skirts long and their corsets on, and stick to riding a tricycle. The more daring bicyclers wanting the thrills and (possible) spills of the Ordinary generally fashioned variations of an ensemble of circus-style tights, short coverings on the upper thighs, and bodysuits or long jackets called sacques.

This culture vs. comfort difficulty is clearly outlined in the outfits of Elsa von Blumen, the bicycle racing contemporary of Louise Armaindo. Louise was frequently called out for scanty and scandalous clothing choices, while Elsa was always complimented on her supposedly demure and modest attire. Paradoxically, Elsa's outfits were always more form fitting than Louise's. When Elsa got on a bike around 1880-1881, she came up with what she dubbed a "full riding costume" that she likely thought would meet with public (press) approval.

The earliest photos of Louise, on the other hand, showed her in a loose black jersey dress buttoned to the throat and falling mid-thigh, with panels of white lace at the throat and cuffs. Her baggy black leggings buttoned at the knee, her socks were a black and white check, her shoes low, almost mannish, and plain black. Her "costume" was altogether more somber, less fine, and less fancy than Elsa's, and minus the little fringed skirt. Soon Louise donned a more fitted, thigh-high jacket dress—the sacque—and "mouse-coloured" tights. She showed no more bare skin than Elsa, but her attire in later photos had a circus vibe.

According to contemporary author Sarah A. Chrisman, who wears Victorian attire 365 days a year and wrote the historical bicycle novel series *Tales of Chetzemoka*, photos of Louise from the period suggest she wore a corset or some type of waist-slimming device under her bicycle outfits. (Chrisman views corsets as empowering rather than oppressive, and she is an enthusiastic rider of an 1880s tricycle.) In the years when Louise and Elsa were endurance racers in strenuous multi-day physical tests, it seems hard to imagine racing for hours, and then days on end, laced into a diaphragm-constricting device.

Careful attention to the pictorial record further suggests that for the greatest part of the late 1870s, all of the 1880s and at least the first half of the 1890s, the majority of female bicyclist chose long skirts, whether wheeling by tricycle or (after about 1887) by safety bicycle. During this same time frame, men's bicycle costumes ranged from minimalist, tight and underwear-like tights for racing, to formal knickerbockers and well-tailored jackets members of clubs favored for city cycling.

By 1887, the number of women riding tricycles in Washington D.C. was considered to be approximately 1,000. That's a fine potential market for the new, dropped frame safety for women which Mrs. Smith rode down Pennsylvania Avenue. And as these new safety bicycle riders took to the road, their idea of how to dress for cycling and the ideas of the rational dress movement converged. At first, The Rational Dress Society, under the leadership of a Lady Florence Harberton, promoted the idea of a divided skirt. Once you tucked the two separate legs of this skirt into boot tops, it was really akin to very baggy, generous knickerbockers, i.e. bloomers. Hearing about a divided skirt made it seem innocuous, though. When the newspapermen finally actually looked closely at Florence Harberton's ensemble, they squawked about how unfeminine the garment was.

In that altogether strange year of 1889, truly a transition year for biking, something shifted. Paging through the popular cycling magazines of the time, the high-wheeled Ordinary was still being sold, and ridden, and raced upon, at the same time that there were many safety bikes out on the market. Psyche, an anonymous female writer who transitioned from the tricycle to a safety bike that year, captured many of her early experiences in letters to *The Wheel and Cycling Trade Review*. Psyche was quick to realize as she moved from trike to bike that she wanted more freedom in a bicycle costume. "Of course, every woman wants to look well on the wheel," she said. "That is certainly not accomplished when the wheelwoman comes to the fray with draperies, reeds, and too narrow skirts." (Psyche is likely referring to woven skirt bustles when she says "reeds.") She recommended a design that was basically a corduroy smock dress over knickerbockers. Short newspaper articles took note of young ladies in these Bloomer-esque outfits riding their safety bicycles.[27]

By the following year—1890—more and more mentions of "bicycle costume" begin to appear in both the bicycle press and daily newspapers. To be "proper" the costume still needed to include a recognizable skirt. The ridiculous balancing act that women had to make comes clear in an article in *The St. Louis Post-Dispatch*, which reports in May that "Fair Bicyclers" are increasing on the streets of the city and that many women are already experts. The report lauds St. Louis women, the report stated, for starting the very first U.S. club of the "Ladies' League of American Wheelmen" (ironic in itself). But when the article showed a drawing of a ladies' safety bike and demonstrated how to mount it, it used the figure of a man dressed in knickerbockers! The lady riders all wore skirts (if divided) and the paper opined: "Another feature of this popular exercise is its modesty. The bar removed from the wheel allows the drapery of the wheelwoman to fall chastely and modestly toward the ground."[28]

One pioneer of the dress reform movement, Annie Jenness-Miller, opined that all the ostentatious elements of that era's fashion were in some way designed to keep women subservient, but she designed a bicycle costume that had a divided skirt *under* a modesty overskirt. She did innovate "leglettes," a kind of one-piece union suit with legs for women, as a petticoat replacement.

As time went on, and more and more women rode in the early 1890s, the skirts, with pantaloons, knickers, or bloomers underneath, got shorter. French women were first to make the skirts really short and jaunty, though of course Elsa had already demonstrated to American women how it could be done.

By the spring of 1894, courageous women such as Chicago's Miss Lucy Porter abandoned the pretense of a skirt altogether. Lucy put on a jacket and generously cut bloomer/knickerbockers and faced her critics. "I was not the recipient of any insulting attention until we reached the outskirts of the city, when a group of silly, half-grown boys indulged in cat-calls. But I had got my courage up by that time," she told the *Chicago Tribune* on April 15, 1894.[29] Porter noted how much faster she could ride and how much lighter her wheel felt, though it must be said that what she and the *Tribune* called "trousers" would be seen by contemporary eyes as pantaloons or bloomers: very roomy, lots of material, and mostly hiding the outline of the legs. She wanted to wear the outfit to ride to her work as a stenographer, and only slip a skirt back on for her working hours.

Florence Harberton had led the way with the divided skirt. Some women like Hartford, Connecticut's Mrs. George D. Johnson made the switch to skirt-free pants after an accident of tangling of skirts in a wheel. Mrs. Johsnon asked the 25 other women in her Hartford riding club to copy her post-tangle design—loose, "Turkish" trousers which gathered at the knees and tan-colored leather leggings down to the boots—and commit to wearing it for a few weeks.[30]

And different cities had different modesty levels. In Buffalo, New York, in late 1894, nearly the entire Women's Wheel and Athletic Club enthusiastically ordered "reformed" bloomer costumes for the following season, and by reformed they meant with skirts over their pantaloons, and in some cases, additional petticoats under the skirts. As "peak bicycle" approached in 1895 and beyond, more and more young women ventured out in their bloomer/knickerbocker outfits without a skirt, following Miss Porter's lead. These outfits' hidden benefit was that they made a diamond-frame bicycle possible for women riders.

There was still social censure ahead; the bloomer or knickerbocker was frequently deemed ugly and ungainly. The costume still necessitated yards and yards of extra material cinched in at waist and calf. It presupposed the woman was wearing a corset, and a shirtwaist or jacket with poofy oversized mutton sleeves. But for the courageous bicyclist at least there was an alternative choice to the skirt and an alternative bike to the drop frame. And just as conservative critics got used to seeing young women in these outfits out on the streets, along came Kittie Knox to really challenge the status quo.

Kittie

In July, 1895 in Waltham, Massachusetts, a contest at the local "athletic carnival" drew a big crowd—over 5,000 people. Amongst the bicyclers, attention was focused on Katherine T. "Kittie" Knox as she took first prize in the costume contest. Her outfit consisted of bloomer-style pants in a checkered tweed, a thigh-length "sack coat" and a cap and gaiters. The newspapers announced her prize with the headline "Bloomers Win" meaning bicycle pants were predicted to be the costume of choice over conventional skirts that year. The men in the grandstand however, the newspapers said, roundly hissed Kittie and all those female riders who didn't have skirts on.[31]

Was it because of the natty pants, or were the disapproval and the catcalls racially oriented? Kittie was mixed-race, born in 1874 to a white mother and a black father, and newspapers of the time referred to her by the epithets "colored" or "mulatto." Just a week after the Waltham contest, Kittie tried to show off her award-winning outfit in Asbury, New Jersey. She rode up to the courtyard where the League of American Wheelmen (LAW) was holding their annual meet in Asbury and did a few loops, her winning ribbon pinned to the lapel of her outfit jacket. She was a card-carrying LAW member (and also a member of Boston's local Riverside Cycle Club), but when she presented her credentials at the check-in table, the "gentleman" in charge refused to recognize them.

Some newspapers seemed to approve that she didn't press the point with LAW officials, though she also didn't leave the gathering. According to different sources, Kittie had difficulty finding a boarding room, though the next day she went on a League ride. The *Asbury Park Press* made an exceedingly strange description of her, noting Kittie "handled her wheel like a witch."[32]

The refusal to let Kittie into the Asbury gathering was considered by some to be unwarranted, and Kittie's case quickly became a race and gender lightning rod, as almost one year earlier the LAW constitution had been amended "so as to provide that only white amateur wheelmen could become members" as the *Louisville Courier Journal* put it. The Louisville, Kentucky faction of the LAW had lobbied hard and long for the measure to disallow African Americans, but there was disagreement internally over the new color bar. And in spite of the color bar, someone within the League had renewed—not canceled—Kittie's membership, even though the constitution had been amended, because her credentials were noted to be up to date at Asbury (she'd been a member since 1893). Parenthetically, the LAW's new language excluded all women—anyone who wasn't a white amateur wheel*man*—though the many white women at the Asbury meet weren't barred from entry.

Historian Lorenz Finison traced Kittie's history and found she was a talented seamstress who took up cycling in her teens and also quickly demonstrated talent in century rides and racing. She gained renown in the Boston area with the Riverside Bike Club, of which she was a member. But when Miss Knox showed off her bicycle garb at the Asbury meet, the simmering dispute within the LAW erupted. The *New York Times* said Kittie was so pretty all the men were "dancing in attendance" around her. But an article in the August 1895 *Southern Cycler* magazine called her a "murky goddess of Beanville several checks shy of the complexion requirement."[33]

There were reports that nine out of ten LAW members supported her, while Southern papers like the *Louisville Courier* lauded her exclusion. The notoriety didn't seem to keep her back, though bicycle advocate Yolanda Overstreet-Davis, who researched Kittie's life for a documentary film, told the author she felt sure the racism was stressful for black bicyclists. The following year, 1896, Kittie was featured in the *Boston Post* as a "champion woman scorcher" and shown riding a diamond-frame bike in her pants suit. The *Post* claimed Kittie was "known everywhere" and would be welcome at any racing track if not for the LAW's edict against women racers. The newspaper described her as out on her wheel every Sunday to the great admiration and envy of her sister riders.

Knox died less than five years after winning the prize for best costume—succumbing to kidney disease at the very young age of 26. Historian Finison, through his work and contact with her family, helped bring Knox and her story back from obscurity. She received a new headstone in the cemetery where she was buried, and her story was told in Finison's book *Boston's Cycling Craze, 1880—1900: A Story of Race, Sport, and Society*.

Out for a Ride

A bloomer outfit could now be seen amongst the throngs of bicyclists out for a pleasure ride on Sundays on Riverside Drive in New York City. But a study of the pictorial record, both illustrations and photos, suggests that an equal number or even a majority of women still chose a skirt when joyriding.

Take for example, Mrs. F.M. Cossitt. The New York press gave her credit for being the first woman to ride a bicycle in New York, and also identified her as an early adopter of the drop-bar safety bicycle. Knowing what we know of how many women tried to ride velocipedes and high wheels, Mrs. Cossitt likely wasn't really the first.

Wife of Franklin Millard Cossitt, Carrie Estella Grey Cossitt learned to ride after her marriage in 1886. An ex-captain of the Riverside Wheelmen club, F.M. enjoyed bicycling with his bride in Central Park or along the tree-lined and bike-crowded Riverside Drive, where frequent park benches made it easy for wheelers to stop, rest, and people watch.

In a photo of her archived at the Museum of New York, Carrie is outfitted in a long skirt, made most likely of a medium dark tricot or corduroy fabric to hide the dirt and dust—it had a very full, pleated design with a minimum of trimmings. Her jacket was matching with tight fitting wrists and a bow decorating the collar front. Gloves and a smart hat complete the ensemble.

Mrs. Cossitt was one of a dozen women to ride in the 1896 Asbury Park annual century run from Newark to Asbury Park (her sister Jennie was the first woman to arrive at the 100-mile mark) and she was also listed as a member of the Riverside Wheelmen.

A number of cycling seamstresses were busy during this period in England and North America trying to patent improvements to women's bicycling costumes. Most of these involved complicated mechanisms to raise and lower skirts for on-bike and off-bike, converting them to lengths that were safe from the maw of the chain, and then back to socially acceptable when a woman stepped off the bike. Underneath a simple A-line shirt and built into the seams was clever riggings both in front and back to draw the middle of the skirt upward but have it still drape out over the wearer's hip. As author Kat Jungnickel notes in her book *Bikes and Bloomers: Victorian Women Inventors and their Extraordinary Cycle Wear*, one of the most fascinating aspects of the designs was that the conversion infrastructures were hidden, keeping the bicycling identity of anyone wearing the skirts incognito.

By this time, in American cities both large and small, bicycling was becoming normalized. For women, the bike's influence went beyond business and pleasure. As *Cosmopolitan* writer Mrs. Reginald de Koven noted in 1895: "To men the bicycle is an unmixed blessing. But to women it is deliverance, revolution, salvation. It is well nigh impossible to overestimate… its influence in the matters of dress and social reform."[34] Mrs. de Koven's articles included two photos of bloomer costumes amongst several other pictures of women in skirts. English women, the article stated, adapted a hunting costume as their pattern for bikewear—knickerbockers or leggings underneath a shorter skirt. French women bicyclists meanwhile got more daring with full on "tight trousers… and all variety of theatrical dress." To Mrs. de Koven, these types of outfits were to be condemned. Convenience was gaining, but modesty was still paramount.[35]

Unsexed by the Bicycle

A t the height of Big Bike—approximately 1895-1897, when endless growth seemed possible—there was a steady flow of press about women's biking. Many newspapers and magazine writers professed to be pro-women and pro-biking, yet there was an underlying anxiety expressed in some articles that bicycling was changing women too much, that the relaxing of corseted figures and the rise of hemlines and the advent of pants would "unsex" women. This was not entirely untrue, if "unsexing" meant to make the definition of female propriety less strict, diverse, and more inclusive.

Some women of the era, like photographer and artist Frances Benjamin Johnston, had already subverted the paradigm that made skirts = femininity. In a self portrait photograph in which she was dressed rather rakishly and yet very convincingly as a male and holding an Ordinary bicycle, Frances conveyed how difficult it was for women to join in on the freedom and pleasure of early bicycling unless in the garb of a man. Physically it was difficult to ride in a long skirt, but the mental/cultural barriers were just as high, and they continued.

Influential writers of the Big Bike era like Maria E. Ward, who published *Bicycling for Ladies* in 1895, worked to keep bicycling in a positive light and to keep the dress code intact. Ward wanted women to ride for enjoyment and exercise and so she lectured on how to avoid social censure. Ward strived to toe that fine line between encouraging women to ride but discouraging them from riding too much, or riding too fast, or riding in inappropriate clothing. The bike gave a woman novel control of her own body and its movement, and the real fear was that women who got a taste of that control would refuse to fulfill the roles of dutiful wife and daughter, not to mention hard-working, self-sacrificing mother. In other words, she'd unsex herself, and on purpose.

To avoid this unsexing, many of the journalists like Ward that chronicled the new wave of bicycling pointedly disapproved of women going fast—"scorching" or racing. Anything beyond sedate and upright pedaling edged into the disapproval zone. Editorial from Mary Sargent Hopkins, who edited *Wheelwoman* magazine through the end of the decade, sought to maintain what she saw as the genteel, aristocratic air of bicycling. She advocated strongly for women's bicycling and yet she simultaneously urged other bicyclists to maintain the prim and proper bicycling status quo. When asked why she didn't support women's racing, Mary Sargent Hopkins replied: "I think it is very much out of place. My work is to convince sensible women that they can ride the wheel gracefully and with propriety." Note the use of the word "grace." Not surprisingly, she condemned bloomers and knickerbockers in favor of skirts and leggings. "If there is one thing I hate," she continued "it is a masculine woman. It has made wheeling just another way for a woman to make a fool of herself."[36]

A few anti-bicycling advocates, including Mrs Lynn Linton and Mrs. Charlotte Smith, used their pens to denounce bicycling for women entirely. Mrs. Linton was not a fan of the modern or new woman that was coming into being in the age of bicycling. She claimed bicycling was "essentially vulgar." Mrs. Smith, president of the Woman's National Rescue League, was a conundrum. She supported equal pay for women and an improvement of working women's lives, yet she poured scorn on the bicycle as promoting "immorality, immodesty, and unwomanly behavior" as Evan Friss puts it in his book *The Cycling City: Bicycles and Urban America in the 1890s.*[37]

Living on quite the opposite side of propriety was Alice Austen, a wealthy, upper class woman from Staten Island who learned photography at age 12 and documented her own life and the lives of her friends through the decades of the 1880s and 1890s. She was chummy with author Maria Ward, as well as Daisy Eliot, the model from the photos in Ward's book *Bicycling for Ladies* (Alice took the photos for the book). During her lifetime she never attempted to make a living from photography, even when she became economically destitute after the stock market crash of 1929. Instead, Alice was more interested in capturing her own life and times. Her photos have a free, refreshing quality compared to many of the stiff compositions in photographs of this era. Those photos of her friends on their bikes convey the feeling that bicycling was normal, natural, joyful. You can almost feel in Alice Austen's shots the turn from Victorian mores and the beginning of the glide through the Edwardian age toward modernity. Alice Austen lived unconventionally with her loving companion Gertrude Tate for over 50 years, and in her photos their union also comes across as normal and modern—quite a feat for a woman born in 1866.

The common immoral "danger" that threatened female riders was seat masturbation, although it wasn't always described with that word. As Ellen Gruber Garvey noted in her book *The Adman in the Parlor*, women were not supposed to ride astride *anything*—from a toy stick horse to a bicycle—that might awaken their sexual selves and give them genital pleasure or take their virginity. Because faster riding might cause faster pleasure from the warmth and the friction, a woman scorching was worse than a man doing so. Supposedly, young women indulging in this bicycle vice would show a certain expression on their faces which physicians in the know could detect. Sitting upright on a drop frame safety instead of hunched over a diamond frame was supposed to help guard against pleasure in the saddle, so manufacturers of safety cycles such as the Rambler in their advertising alluded to the "erect and graceful" position their bicycle encouraged.[38]

Doctors also thought the bicycle would interfere with women's ability to bear children—the ultimate unsexing. In the 1897 book *Women and the Bicycle*, Dr. E.D. Page condemned the bike for building up leg muscles more than other muscles, for interfering with the freedom of respiration (though how it could do so more than a corset was not addressed), and claimed that riding could displace the uterus or cause the pelvis in young girls to grow malformed. Lastly Dr. Page accused bicycling of giving young women an easy means of transportation that would encourage them to slip out of grasp of their chaperones and go to public houses where they or their reputations would be ruined.

Sex workers of the era were sometimes accused of using the bicycle to promote their businesses and find new clients. *The Week* magazine claimed in 1897 that Parisian sex workers took to the bicycle so that they could wheel around and look for clientele while also being able to race away from Parisian policemen who might ask them for their registration documents. In 1896 in Cincinnati, Ohio, police were surprised one evening when a woman pedaled past them in a white dress and they recognized her as the brothel owner "Madam Mitchell." She fled the officers, but when she had to stop for a streetcar the policemen arrested her—not for riding a bicycle but for the sin/crime of leaving the city's designated red-light district.[39]

CHAPTER FIVE

Racing to the Finish Line
(1894-1902)

Londonderry Annie

I n the last five years of the nineteenth century, so
many women rode bicycles that daring feats became
more and more common. It was part of the culture
and the *fin de siecle* times for men and women, and
especially those trying for an economic jackpot, to take
chances, dares, attempt outlandish feats. But even so, the

bravado of Annie Cohen Kopchovsky, known as Annie Londonderry, seemed extraordinary.

Annie gained copious press recognition when she started to ride around the world on a bicycle in the summer of 1894. A married mother of three, Annie left her children and her husband, and her job selling advertising for Boston newspapers, for a 15-month bicycle trek from July 1894 to October 1895. Annie told newspapers the purpose of the trip was to win a $10,000 bet. The evidence for this wager is rather thin, according to her biographer and grand-nephew Peter Zheutlin. Zheutlin thoroughly researched Annie's travels and concluded that she was not only a great adventurer—gutsy, bold, and inventive—she was also a superior marketer, larding her tales with fanciful, mostly invented detail.

Annie, like Louise Armaindo before her, was practicing press relations and that era's version of social media. She got the Londonderry water company to sponsor her as she biked, using Londonderry as her surname; she sold postcards with her picture to generate cash; and she even created a magic lantern presentation with staged photos highlighting dramatic (fabricated) moments of her journey. She knew instinctively that people were fascinated in what she wore while on her bicycle journey. Over the course of her 15 months away from home she moved gradually from traditional heavy skirts and undergarments to a bloomer costume to an even further pared down, men's style pants-and-jacket ensemble.

Zheutlin began to research his great-aunt's ride in 2003 and found many discrepancies between newspaper reports of Annie's trek by bike and what he could discern as the true steps of Annie's voyage. Her transportation included quite a bit of train and ship travel, and many fewer miles on the bike than what was reported. Many of the stories that she told in her presentations couldn't be corroborated, or had lots of contradictory details when fact checked by Zheutlin. She eventually, after some exhausting stretches, managed to return to Chicago, and wrote a series of newspaper articles about her trip. She started to write a book (though didn't finish it), stayed married to her husband, and settled back to life as wife and mother. In spite of the fanciful spin and tall tales, this globe-trotting woman bicyclist still managed something extraordinary, and came back with a great tale to tell of adventure and many miles of bicycling. Annie died in 1947.

Tillie and Dottie Race to the Finish

In the 1880s Louise Armaindo had helped make women's bicycle racing—on high-wheel Ordinary bikes—an exciting spectacle, but it couldn't be called an established sport. By the middle of the 1890s, with ample backing from investors, sophisticated velodromes (steeply banked, wooden oval arenas for track cycling) had sprung up in cities all over the United States and Canada, from Winnipeg to St. Louis to San Francisco.

It was men's bicycle racing that was the main event at these velodromes. By popular demand, however, a group of truly amazing athletic women also began to race in six-day and other races on the new safety cycles and in front of big crowds.

Dottie Farnsworth and Tillie Anderson were two racers whose stories reveal the turbulence and the excitement of this time. Both Dottie and Tillie were from the Midwest, the most popular region for women's racing, and both learned to ride and race on safety bikes. (Few of the women of the 1889 high-wheel races—Helen Baldwin was a notable exception—made the transition from high-wheel to safety racing.) Tillie was born in 1875 in Sweden and emigrated to the U.S. as a teen, landing in Chicago. An accomplished seamstress, Tillie saved for a year to buy her first bicycle. When her beau Philip Anderson realized the extent of her cycling talent, he abandoned his own budding bicycle racing career to coach hers. It was a winning strategy, as Tillie seldom lost her races. Dottie Farnsworth, born Leona Marie Farnsworth in 1873, was always a ferocious challenger to Anderson's golden record. Both rode from around 1895 to just into the new first decade of the twentieth century. For those years they accrued accolades and won races, trained as hard as men racing, and stayed in shape through the fickle public's up and down response to racing and the difficulty promoters had in organizing lucrative women's races.

Colonel Albert Pope of the Columbia Bicycle Co.—and a huge supporter of the League of American Wheelmen (LAW)—viewed racing as a marketing tool to sell more cycles to women. Thus he was amenable to sponsoring female racers. But former bicycle racer George D. Gideon, who headed up the League's racing rules department in the 1890s, was a foe of women's bike racing as sport—and he wasn't alone. Many mainstream gentlemen riders along with Gideon were of the opinion that American women could ride bicycles—preferably tricycles and then safeties—but women racing bicycles was visually displeasing and morally questionable, part of the breakdown of mores and the "unsexing" of women. Gideon was outspoken in his idea that women's racing ruined the reputation and professionalism of male cycle racing and bicycling in general, and he pressed the LAW to blacklist the velodromes that allowed women's races.

Because of its popularity with the public, women's racing continued, especially in the Midwest. It was exciting for viewers at the velodrome to see women such as Tillie and Dottie work hard, win races, and go on to become known entities. Strong racing women could draw local crowds eager to see their homegrown heroines speeding around raised wooden tracks in aerodynamic outfits complete with skin tight "leggings," striped stockings, and body-revealing jerseys. The outfits were part of the thrill for attendees, there was no doubt. Much more color and pizazz in the women's outfits than in men's racing costumes made women's races a novel titillation. But this feature—the pageantry of the outfits and the novelty—caused tut-tutting from factions who wanted women to be more docile, decorous, and dressed accordingly.

Plucky isn't a word much used at present, but in the early 1890s it was a popular way to describe women who insisted on racing their bikes. Many men and male journalists admired the women who trained and toiled and rode and sometimes won races. But plucky was a code word similar to "graceful"—in plucky's case it was a useful descriptor of the courage required for women to test their own endurance, yet it was sometimes deployed as a stand-in for other less admiring words, such as "uppity" or "aggressive" or "not graceful."

Going back to that key year, 1889, it was clear that long before the safety bicycle, women had been capable of mastering a wheel. They had plenty of natural talent. But this talent wasn't acceptable to those that thought women racers were a threat to the respectability of bicycle racing rather than an enticing enhancement. It was in part a culture and a class issue—most of the female racers were not of the leisure class. Instead, they were using their athleticism to survive and develop physically and financially. Thus, the League of American Wheelmen did its race-killing work mostly behind the scenes in an ongoing effort to stifle the women—already less powerful than their male counterparts—who dared race.

As the safety era developed, however, shrewd (or progressive, or greedy) promoters of bicycle racing did their best to attempt to skirt the LAW and create a prosperous racing franchise. They might not have been in it for female emancipation, and in fact could be ruthless and exploitive, but they nevertheless aided the cause.

By the end of the decade even more fresh female talent was aspiring to race, many of the women coming from abroad. Though there was similar public disapproval of women racers in France and England, there was also public interest and support. A French racer with the stage name Lisette (real name Amelie Le Gall) garnered a lot of newspaper ink and came to the U.S, providing some needed fresh competition to Tillie and Dottie.

Meanwhile the LAW continued on its quiet determination to shut down women's racing by blacklisting tracks that insisted on holding the popular events. This destabilized women racers' already precarious ability to make a living with racing and keep going. A few cities, notably Minneapolis and Canada's Winnipeg, were havens for racing. Tillie earned various nicknames such as the "Terrible Swede," "Champion of America" and "Chicago Lass" and she was the grand dame of this underreported and suppressed sport.

Dottie, called the "American Whirlwind," was the perpetual underdog nipping at Tillie's back fender, perennially getting second place wins to Tillie's first place medals. In a six-day race in Chicago in 1896, Tillie and Dottie were bike by bike to the last laps, until Tillie pulled ahead by one-seventeenth of a mile in the home stretch, receiving a "boisterous" ovation. In a six-day race in 1897 Tillie had to spurt for the entire last hour to keep just ahead of Dottie as well as Helen Baldwin. All three had 264 miles and 14 laps and Tillie cycled full-speed and flat out to nose ahead of the other two just at the finish. It's not unthinkable that these races were all fixed—the women's handlers and managers were no strangers to underhanded dealings, and the lack of LAW approval and oversight didn't help. For example, Choppy Warburton, coach to the French racer known as Lisette, was especially known for darker deeds, encouraging his athletes with liquid doses from a little black bottle long before elite racers were accused of doping.

But what none of the racers or the handlers could foresee was that Dottie's tragic death after flying off a "cycle dazzle" or "cycle whirl" while she was touring with the Walter L. Main circus in 1902 would lead to an abrupt end to this era of American female cycle racing. Poor Dottie! She was known for her fearlessness on the track and her ferocity. In fact, sometimes the press took her to task for pushing too hard and perhaps elbowing her fellow female racers in the heat of competition. In 1902 she was touring to make money between racing seasons. She veered disastrously off the cycle whirl and crashed on the sidelines. Her internal injuries and then peritonitis conspired to kill her a few days later.

Tillie fared altogether better—though her husband died that same year, 1902, of tuberculosis. Tillie traded on her good bicycling record, having enough economic wherewithal to build a second career as a massage therapist. She died in 1965, and was inducted (posthumously) into the Cyclists Hall of Fame.

Even before Dottie's death there were broader hints that the LAW's efforts were succeeding at squelching women's bicycle racing. When a race was planned in Rochester in February, 1902 the paper reported: "Rochester Will Shortly Hold Freak Event Which Should Be Stopped."[40] That race did manage to go on—with Tillie Anderson in the line-up—and Syracuse, New York cyclist May Allen won. But women's bicycle racing now faced an additional foe: the automobile.

Women's racing and its suppression was just one aspect of a larger set of societal and cultural shifts. The bicycle boom of the early 1890s peaked with production of just over a million bicycles in 1899. Bicycling would experience many ups and downs over the coming decades, but the production downturn right at the shift of the millennium meant the bike industry began and continued to lose ground to the slow-rising popularity of the car. Many of the tinkerers and inventors working in bicycle innovation had decamped to auto development. And all those beautiful bike roads the LAW helped to build for bicycling were just perfect for the shiny new automobiles. Those roads definitely aided in kicking bicycles to the curb. But first, before most bicyclists had any idea of the change that was coming, an outburst of speed and pluck by a variety of intrepid women gave the last days of the first bike boom some added interest.

Dora, then Margaret

In Colorado, married bicyclist Dora Rinehart started riding her bike in the early 1890s and found she was somewhere between a cycle tourist and an endurance racer. Born in 1863, Dora Ellen Moore used her married name, Mrs. A.E. Rinehart, when she rode—though she never seemed to have her husband photographer A.E. Rinehart as sidekick. Instead she started solo 100-mile century rides and got a little addicted to them. At first male century enthusiasts were amused—the secretary of the Century Road Club laughed in 1896 when Rinehart suggested she wanted to beat his record of doing 132 centuries in a year. But as one newspaper commented: "It is sometimes a dangerous thing to laugh at a woman, even such an amiable one as the average wheelwoman. Mrs. Rinehart then and there swore inwardly that she would bring her list of centuries to the hundred notch by the end of the year."[41]

Rinehart rode 20 centuries in 20 consecutive days and one day rode from Denver to Colorado Springs—then back, and back again. At the end of the year Rinehart had won two accolades—third place among Coloradans for number of miles ridden in 1896 (her total was 17,173), and first place for number of 100-mile rides (116). The newspaper bestowed the title "America's Greatest Cyclienne" on Rinehart.

Her wins also generated backlash from those against female bike equality. In 1898, from an interview in her new home in Syracuse, New York, Dora expressed outrage that the Associated Cycling Clubs of New York proposed to bar women from century runs. "The statement that century runs are very harmful to women does not agree with my experience or observation," Rinehart noted. "A women century rider is no more apt to suffer from the long rides, in my opinion, than a man."[42] Associated Cycling Clubs tried to recycle that tired argument that women degraded men's rides.

As was the norm, many reporters of Dora's feats were just as fascinated by the woman's clothing and appearance as by her stamina. Dora favored a divided skirt—we'd call it a culotte, or wide-legged pants—of "blue woolen goods" and a blue and yellow sweater and matching cap. The divided skirt was something of a concession garment—not as chaste as a skirt, not as scandalous as pants—and it is telling that Rinehart once admitted that on long unobserved stretches "in the suburbs," where she wouldn't be seen, she changed into a pair of knickerbockers.

Rinehart's first bicycle was a drop frame, though she also used a diamond-frame bicycle. Videographer Jim Kellett believed Dora left her husband A.E. for another male bicyclist—in any case little more is heard from Dora after 1897. She died in obscurity in Minnesota in 1943. By 1898 another woman, Mrs. M.S. Allen of Worcester, Mass., broke Dora's record by doing 117 centuries and over 20,000 miles in the saddle.

As the nineteenth century gave way to the twentieth, strong bicycling women were more commonplace and more extreme. Daring deeds—faster, longer rides—were expected to get a person into the newspaper or get them a sponsorship like the one Annie Londonderry solicited for her round-the world travel. Racing had a stigma, but one area that still fascinated the press and thus the public, giving women room to participate, was endurance bicycling.

Born in Bavaria in 1876 as Margareta Nagengast, Margaret Gast immigrated to the United States around the time of her 16th birthday and settled in New York City just as the bicycle was gaining widespread popularity. She learned to ride in the 1890s along with tens of thousands of other New Yorkers. Soon bike clubs she rode with realized Margaret had an almost superhuman endurance. Giving her the moniker "Little Duchy," the clubs entered her in races. She started to win, and the longer she rode, the better she performed.

She began to train for a "diamond century"—a slog of ten 100-mile rides—on a triangle-shaped set of dirt roads in rural Long Island where cyclists liked to rack up the miles. She wasn't the first female cyclist to try this form of endurance riding; Louise Armaindo was fond of similar endurance displays, and a Long Island hotel called Valley Stream had seen a few other female athletes use the back roads and the 20-mile loop to amass centuries.

Margaret set her first record in 1900, bicycling the incredible distance of 1,000 miles in 99 hours. Rain, wind, and copious amounts of mud plagued her in the first days, but once she had 1,000 miles under her wheels she found endurance reserves, and in that same year went on to finish 20 centuries in 222 hours and five minutes. Gast was entered in the record books for the fastest 2,000 miles on a bike by man or woman.

After setting that record, which meant she had biked 2,000 miles in nine days with only a few hours of sleep, Margaret Gast declared to the gathered newspapermen that the main reason to ride a bike was for the profit. That must have been a sleep-deprived sardonic aside, as she didn't receive any (reported) pay for that epic ride. For some years she did support herself with feats of endurance bicycling, but it was no easy living. Looking back years later she admitted:

"I did want to be known as the Champion Woman Cyclist of America."[43]

For what would be her final Long Island endurance ride, Margaret was doggedly determined, and had gotten to 25 century rides, bicycling on a safety cycle with a light so that she could continue to rack up the miles at night. But some of the people living in the villages along the route were dismayed and even scandalized by Gast's black bloomers and orange-and-blue-striped jersey, and by the extreme determination she demonstrated. Eventually, after she fell a few times in full view of the media entourage, public opinion turned against her quest. A local sheriff intervened. With over 2,500 miles done, Gast begged to be allowed to complete the century ride she had in progress. While the local Nassau County district attorney said in a statement that he considered it "improper, immoral, and illegal to make such an exhibition on the public highways," the sheriff Abraham Furman allowed her to complete 2,600 miles. But after that, Nassau County prohibited "continuous century performances" by women.[44] One paper called her "Ghastly Miss Gast" in disgust, reporting without specific proof that cocaine was injected into her body in order to help her keep up with the ride.[45]

When she finally stopped wheeling she had accrued a total of 2,600 miles in 12 days, eight hours, and 55 minutes. With this long-distance record set, Margaret called herself a champion, and she went on to win a six-day bicycle race, then subsequently took to the circus to capitalize on her successes. She did speed stunt riding in the "amusement saucers" (tiny portable board tracks) that were very similar to the cycle dazzle that claimed her contemporary Dottie Farnsworth's life in 1902. Margaret appeared to be self-reliant and pragmatic—she did her own mechanical repairs and when it seemed clear the motor was not just a novelty she took up a bare-bones motorcycle along with the moniker "Mile a Minute Gal." She survived a spectacular motorcycle crash on a Palm Beach, Florida course and yet kept stunt riding until 1922, when she became a masseuse and physical therapist, opening a women's spa in New York. She died in 1969 and was inducted into the Bicycling Hall of Fame in 1993.

While there was still an amateur women's bicycle race here and there after Dottie's death in 1902, in general the era of women's racing had ended. There's no proof that a strong women's bike racing industry, with promoted and supported stars, would have saved biking's downfall. Yet the more recent bicycle craze of the 1960s to 1970s, commonly attributed to the Tour de France, shows it's not a completely far fetched idea. Bike racing for men, especially men's six day races, was still tremendously popular in the opening decade of the 20th century.

CHAPTER SIX

REACHING OUT FOR MORE SALES

From Bike to Car, or Boys and Their Toys (1900-1920)

Reinvention #2

Cycling 1.0's zenith is often pinned at 1895, and by that year an estimated four million Americans had a bicycle. Yet advances in bicycle technology, and the mass consumer market in bikes that built up and thrived for a few years, was on a cresting wave. In the spring of 1896, scores of the newer bike manufacturers collapsed, a casualty of excess supply and shaky finances. Concurrently, bike engineers pushed forward what was, for them, a logical next step—

engines on bikes and carriages. The automobile was getting ready to (slowly, but steadily) engulf hearts and minds.

Keeping up with the neighbors began to mean coveting and eventually owning an automobile. Even Colonel Pope of Columbia Bicycles—who said women were a key to biking's long-term health, and who made multiple determined efforts through advertising to convince women they could ride "without sacrifice of dignity or personal attractiveness," as William Bancroft, publisher of *Outing*, put it in 1905 – eventually threw in his lot with the automobile.[46] And much of the advertising that so fueled the bike's popularity with women in the "90s turned, in the new century, to emphasizing technical features over fashionability.

Car prominence wasn't built in a day or even in a decade. People didn't stop riding their bicycles overnight. Women didn't stop hankering for the personal freedom the bicycle was providing. But during the decade from 1895 to 1905, ideas of modernity, man's power over nature, and manifest destiny floated in the American air. Alongside this was the suffragette/ suffragist movement urging for womens' right to vote, and the counter-effort by the powerful to suppress this desire. Mix this with the crash of bike manufacturing, the oppression of women's racing, and the ambitions of Henry Ford, and you have some strong forces putting the brakes on the bicycle's role.

When you look a little closer at the years and then decades after the first huge peak of bicycling, it becomes clearer that there were smaller, continuing cycles of boom and bust: the teens and period of WWI saw a little spike upward; the Depression renewed interest in bicycling; WWII caused another surge; and the 1970s saw new hordes of bicyclists inspired by the Tour de France and spurred by oil price shocks, before the 1980s set off mountain bike mania.

Esther Pohl Lovejoy and Liverpool Liz

The cultural forces of the century's turn meant different things to different women bicyclists. In the case of a strong ambitious cyclist like Margaret Gast looking to support herself, those forces may have nudged her toward a motorcycle to show off her endurance feats. The motorized bicycle was a way to get faster, to keep up with the men.

But what about someone like Oregon physician Esther Pohl Lovejoy?

Born in a logging camp in 1869, Esther was tough and ambitious. She worked in a dry-goods emporium in order to pay for a three-year training at the University of Oregon Medical Department (UOMD) to become a doctor. In a short memoir of her time in medical school for the Oregon Historical Quarterly[47] Esther noted that she and the other medical students walked from the end of the streetcar line to school as they were all struggling students and there weren't, she said, any bicycles around (approximately 1890). Just a few years later Esther had bought a bicycle to increase her mobility as a doctor. In a biography by Kimberly Jensen, Esther's friend and journalist Nan Strandborg recalled that by the time she was a young doctor (around 1894-1895) she would bicycle around east Portland to births with her bicycle rigged to carry her obstetrical supplies.[48]

As a woman doctor, Pohl Lovejoy had to hustle to get her patients—people had reservations about her youth and her gender. But she had a secret advantage—a friend in the telephone operators' office who tipped her if someone on the party line had a baby on the way. The bike helped her get efficiently to impending births at all hours.

Ester was often described as an activist for women's health; she was appointed the state's first female head of the city's fledgling health department. Yet somewhere in the 1905-1906 period, the prosperous Pohl Lovejoy left behind her specially-equipped bicycle, and went on to purchase an automobile. It was the ultimate class symbol of modernity and convenience.

Literally on the other side of town in Portland's rough North End, Esther's contemporary Liverpool Liz (Elizabeth

Smith Young) was a saloon owner who bought not one bike, but (reportedly) an entire fleet of them. Liz owned the Senate Saloon at the corner of NW First and Couch Streets in the part of town that sailors frequented. Her second floor was a warren of rooms used by sex workers. Legends and myths about Liz—her ostentatious diamond necklace, how she alternately saved sailors' money by keeping it in her safe and also fleeced some of them by charging them for rounds of champagne for the entire saloon are just two of many anecdotes. The stories are thick with scandalous deeds, and short on substantiating facts.

Fred T. Merrill, Portland's major bicycle merchant, was also a larger-than-life character known to spin a yarn. Merrill was a former bicycle racer and stunt rider (as he told it, he was inspired to be a bicyclist by seeing Carrie Moore do her tricks by bike on her solo trip to Portland). Fred gave his life story to the local Oregonian newspaper decades after the bicycle had fallen from widespread favor. His interviewer was Stewart Holbrook, a local journalist who loved and recorded stories of the city's past.

In Merrill's telling to Holbrook in the 1920s, Liz became a bicycle convert in the mid 1890s and bought the entire fleet of bicycles from him, as well as purchasing land and outfitting a bicycle track—she called it Evergreen Park—in what is now Portland's Peninsula Park (a well-loved rose garden and park on the city's East Side).[49] That Liz owned that land is deemed true; she's on the sale bill to Portland's park department.

Merrill told Holbrook that Liz staged races at her fenced-in "scorcher track" with some of the sex workers from her saloon racing the bikes in her fleet. Holbrook theorized that Liz's cycle track failed because there was a saloon right in the middle of the track, which didn't sit well with, he said, "parents of young cyclists." It is true that neighbors protested this bicycle version of a beer garden by trying to block the permit.[50]

When there weren't races, Fred said, Liz's sex workers would ride around town in their finest (skin-baring) outfits, soliciting customers. "When Blanche Hamilton's girls and Liverpool Liz's girls and all the rest of them took to the wheel, the society girls got off their wheels and went afoot or went back to their buggy," Fred recalled to Holbrook. He said the working women not only had the best bikes, they also had the best outfits, dolled up, and, as he put it "in bright cycling clothes, including the scandalous split skirts… ran all over town ringing their bells and with colored streamers flying."[51]

Fred's theory is intriguing but thus far hasn't been corroborated. Liz's bicycle track failed, and she saw her saloon business also diminish as the sailing trade innovated and steam vessels required far fewer sailors. The story of her band of bicycle babes, if indeed they did bike to advertise their services, is thus far lost to history's fog. It seems more plausible that a number of cultural and marketing forces were favoring the uptake of the automobile while discarding the bicycle. While Esther Pohl Lovejoy suffered the early loss of her first husband and her son in the first years of the new century, her career flourished and she had a long and fruitful life, dying in 1967. Elizabeth Smith Young, aka Liverpool Liz, died of pneumonia in 1913. In a strange footnote, while it is impossible to know if these two women ever met, for their paths were very different, they are buried not far from each other in Portland's Lone Fir cemetery, though Liz's grave is unmarked by a headstone.

Doldrums

The first two decades of the twentieth century are marked by the car's uptake—first by the wealthy elite, and then gradually, more and more by the middle class. During this time, bikes begin to be slowly relegated to, in large part, boys' toys. Bicycle manufacturers can't be blamed for wanting a steady market. They myopically thought their best bet for finding it would be with American boys, and rarely targeted girls in their advertising outreach. In some advertising illustrations a girl looks on admiringly as a boy received a Christmas bike. Thankfully, though, the bicycle was too practical to ever die out completely. And if we peel back the layers of American culture, past the slick magazines and a one-size-fits-all cultural mentality that mainstream media tends to favor, we find that bicycling was still around, and women kept doing it.

In the first decade of the twentieth century, the United States was accepting giant waves of immigrants, experiencing incredible coast-to-coast growth and expansion, as well as undergoing constant societal and technological change.

From 1895-1900 hundreds of thousands of bikes were still sold annually, though sales never equaled the 1895 peak. By 1901, air was leaking from the bike boom's tires; sales and prices plummeted. Bike boosters quickly tried to reverse this. Salesman and bicycling "authority" W.H. Pickens mourned the "decease" of biking in 1901 in a newspaper column, and said that society's "indifference" was killing cycling.

The safety cycle wasn't the new thing anymore, and Pickens claimed that biking's popularity with the "masses" caused high society to look elsewhere for amusement, to eschew watching or participating in bike racing and instead take up golf, and to let their wheels stand "rusting in dark cellars or dusty garrets."[52]

Evan Friss, author of *The Cycling City*, showed that car growth was very slow. In 1902, for example, 580,000 new bicycles found owners—only 23,000 autos did. And there was plenty of open road for bikes by then—154,000 miles of road by 1904.[53] In mass marketing and advertising there was a shift, technologically and psychologically, away from the bicycle; the no-gear two-wheeler didn't have that thrill anymore. A shiny, smoky auto passing by in a cloud of road dust stirred hearts more powerfully than the two-wheeled bike. In the first years of the new century, Colonel Pope tried to create the next big biking "thing" with a chainless drive bicycle. Chainless drive meant the conventional bike's chain and chain ring were replaced by an enclosed and chainless transmission system. The technology did not catch on.

Pope pushed hard on the chainless drive. It had its pluses. The chainless mechanism was completely enclosed, keeping oil away from the rider. It would have been a boon for women in skirts, whose hems very often still skimmed right around the dirtiest part of a bicycle. Its bevel gear system would have helped riders on hills. But you could buy a good-looking ladies' bicycle for $40—could people justify $100 for the chainless drive bike? In spite of ads touting "no chain or guard to catch the skirts," it seemed they couldn't.

The chainless drive really was an innovation that women would have appreciated—and perhaps if women in general enjoyed the economic clout and buying power they do now, the chainless idea would have gotten further. Bloomers— the whole idea of pants—was still controversial by this time. Bloomers' power to titillate as a fashion statement was over. Versions of them were widely used as athletic apparel in gymnasiums and even in swimming costumes. They weren't considered modest enough when it came to street apparel, including bicycling. The photographic evidence seems to point to skirts or divided skirts as de rigeur, though in Europe (and it varied from country to country and between urban areas) bloomers were not as frowned upon.

In this first decade of the 1900s, innovation in bicycle fashion advanced. For example, two women—Caroline E. Miller and Grace T. Heineke—created various versions of dress guards so skirts weren't caught in back wheels; dozens of women patented different ideas for skirts that could be raised for rides, and saddles that conformed better to female anatomy were also patented by a few women.

As the first decade of the new century advanced, bike racers and promoters migrated toward the excitement of car racing, automobile design, and automobile sales. Racer William Morgan, who had raced many times with Louise, became an automobile executive. And John Price, who bested Louise in a race early in her career, became an expert at building car racing tracks. But T.W. Eck, who had been Louise's main coach nearly the entire length of her career, swore to the newspapers in 1907 that bicycle racing was heading for a grand revival.

He had—no surprise—a vested interest. T.W. Eck was always a prodigious promoter and booster. Starting in 1906 he toured the U.S. with a courageous woman cyclist named Lillian Chick and a dangerous though novel bicycle invention he called the "Tom Eck globe"—a wire cage 16 feet in diameter, in which Chick rode very fast on the rollers of a stationary trainer. Once the trainer's rollers were locked, Chick's bicycle would rocket in a loop. Chick seemed fearless on the contraption, and Tom Eck continued to be able to get newspaper coverage for the globe, and presumably crowds to watch, demonstrating that fast feats of derring-do on the bicycle still had the power to attract the public.[54]

A half dozen years later, Eck tried to bring back bicycle racing for women single handedly. He toured in 1913 with a group of first four and then three racers, with a New Jersey woman named Jessie Stelter as his star. The races were billed as pure entertainment, and neither Tom nor Jessie stirred up much interest in women's racing. Mostly, newspapers seemed more fond of asking Eck about past racing glories. He was happy to oblige, and he always mentioned the men he'd trained at length. If he mentioned the women, his interviewers didn't include them in the subsequent articles. It wasn't until nearer his own death in 1922 that newspaper articles began to mention Louise Armaindo, and he then referred to her as the greatest athlete he'd ever known!

In men's bike racing, new technology crept onto the track as racers begin to be paced by the motorized bicycle or motorcycle. Though not all that much is written about the transitionary period between massive bike riding and massive auto uptake, it's clear that the motorbike or motorcycle attracted an ardent following of (mostly) young men who were proud to zoom around on what, at first, were just souped-up motorized bicycles. They made a hellish racket and scorched a lot of tender shin skin. But to the speed-seekers of the new century, like Margaret Gast, the transition from bike daredevilry to motorbike scorching may have seemed natural, modern, and also necessary to make a living.

Boy Toy

By the spring of 1916, the "European" war was getting ready to go global, French designer Coco Chanel made fashion waves with her ideas of simple, sporty dresses with "dropped" waists and hemlines that rose up the shins, while the U.S. magazine *Motorcycle Illustrated* started talking about bicycles... a lot. Bicycle sales enjoyed a modest little swing upward, and sales were domestic as well as to Europe, where bike production had suffered from war's outbreak.

Motorcycle Illustrated absorbed the old *Bicycling World* magazine in 1909 and in its first years was a B-to-B magazine dedicated to the marvel of the motorcycle. But by 1916 the tenor shifted—perhaps editorial staff realized bicycles and motorcycles were selling from the same storefronts in towns and cities. The Goodyear Tire Company shepherded the idea of a "Million Bicycles Campaign" for 1916.

The thrust was to start a young boy lusting after a bike early. He'd be your customer for life, was the thought, graduating over time from two wheels to two wheels plus a motor. Goodyear Tire sponsored bicycle races (but only for men), and bicycle clubs started to spring up again. A bike/moto hybrid called the "Power Bicycle"—basically an early e-bike, though stinkier, made a debut. Margaret Gast rode one in a long coat, fancy hat, and no helmet. The Century Road Club (CRC), founded all the way back in 1891, managed to keep going even when the bicycle market took its turn-of-the-century dive, and the club enjoyed a resurgence, with members attempting to outdo each other in the number of centuries they could manage in a year (and also on one single set of tires).

Women didn't appear to get sustained marketing attention. Instead, in the *Motorcycle Illustrated* of the war period, the most common view of a woman was sitting in a motorcycle sidecar. While many women fought for voting rights and workplace pay equality, and fashion did not revert to the tight corsets and ground-sweeping skirts of twenty-five years earlier, women were still expected to be proper. That meant showing only the approved amount of skin, wearing gloves, keeping their hair long, and putting on a hat in public.

In a *Motorcycle Illustrated* ad from Westfield Manufacturing Company, dealers were exhorted to target women: "It is in your interest to cultivate women prospects to your window displays and by keeping women's bicycles out on the best part of your floor space. And last but not least, be sure that your store and repair shop is not the kind of place that a woman is afraid to enter."[55] But it was clearly still a man's world, whether by bicycle or by motorcycle. White middle-class men were the first to make the bicycle universally popular in the 1870s, and when it became clear that bikes were ubiquitous and cheap enough for nearly anyone to own, white *gentlemen* moved on.

Bike salesmen and jobbers, store owners, and manufacturers were almost all men, and after the downturn from 1895 on, they couldn't figure out how to leverage the wonderful qualities of the bicycle to everybody else. With few exceptions, they focused their sales efforts on bikes to boys and motorcycles to men. From 1900 to 1920, marketing beyond white men was risky, for putting more of an effort into women and other disenfranchised members of society meant cycling could further lose its elitist and masculine appeal, according to the authors of *Cycling and Society*.[56]

By the time America reluctantly entered the war in 1917, bike sales were buoyant, though nothing approaching the '90s boom. The year of the million bicycles didn't even come close—sales were around 526,000 in 1916 and then 606,000 in 1917. The 1917 sales numbers got a boost from the U.S. Government ordering 100,000 bicycles for the war effort.

At the same time the number of cars produced was rising faster, as was the number of automobile registrations. And while Teddy Roosevelt, president from 1901-1909, eschewed the car and advocated for a sporting, masculine, outdoors life which included cycling, after him William Taft celebrated the auto, officially endorsing it in 1909 and filling the White House garage with cars.[57]

From 1917 on, the American economy was performing solidly and the bicycle went along for the ride. New riders such as well-to-do snowbirds going south for winter enjoyed biking on the boulevards of Palm Beach, Florida. Mrs. Jane Yatman Ruch, a pleasure and century rider who was part of this WWI-era biking renaissance, complained to *Motorcycle Illustrated* that manufacturers stopped making suitably-sized diamond frames for women, and she hoped they would remedy this to encourage women riders. "So here's to the bicycle," she said, "May it again become popular among women as it was back in the good old days."[58] Ruch and others like her got back on their bicycles in part because biking was for a short time considered patriotic and pleasurable.

The position of prestige that the bike had held in the 1890s could not be fully replicated, however, and bicycle sales never did bounce back to 1890s levels. Car sales rose while the bike industry failed at the million bikes goal and also failed at finding another coherent strategy that might have allowed the bicycle to really compete on the roads.

Dorothy, Bike Soldier

Born in England at the height of the cycling boom and orphaned at five, Dorothy Lawrence desired a career as a journalist. By the age of 19, she managed to land a few newspaper assignments, but she hadn't found steady employment. It was war time, and despite having no firm job or freelance support from an editor, Dorothy longed to be a war correspondent. Women of her era were nurses, and the first female soldiers were many decades and many wars into the future.

The solution? Dorothy decided to disguise herself as a soldier. To stay inconspicuous while traveling, she would use a bicycle to help her get closer to the fighting.

It was both harder and easier than she at first imagined. She made her way to Paris by boat, accompanied by a ramshackle bicycle she bought for two English pounds. She didn't have a well-defined plan, but biked whenever possible to avoid questions about what she was doing. By 1915 a piece of the war front was not far from the French capital city, and Dorothy found it easy to cycle to the town of Creil, where she looked for help in transforming from lady bicyclist to British soldier boy.

French soldiers and civilians were convinced she was either a nurse or some kind of a war groupie or prostitute; if she said she was not, people could not understand what the "petite Anglaise" was doing trying to get nearer the fighting. Eventually, Dorothy finagled a safe conduct pass to get herself even nearer the French front, and she bicycled to a small town called Senlis. When her safe conduct expired, she hid in a forest and left her bike in a shed.

Following some torturous, buggy nights of little sleep, Dorothy realized she was not closer to any goals, either getting a needed uniform or slipping into an actual regiment. So she pedaled back to Paris. She was still determined to make it to the front, so she pleaded with British soldiers she met on the street to help her put together the needed pieces of a uniform. Over a number of weeks, she put together what she thought she needed from packages the soldiers handed over under the pretense she was doing their laundry for money.

Making a well-fitting uniform was an undertaking. Dorothy wrapped her breasts in bandages and padded her back to make it fill out the jacket. She cropped her long dark hair. When she left for the front at a town called Béthune on her bicycle, she was fully kitted but without necessary ID tags.

On the road she met a sapper (soldier-engineer) she felt she could trust and told him her ambition. Sapper "Dunn" helped her hide in bombed-out cottages, and then took her on his night shifts when he was setting trench mines. After just ten days, Dorothy began to suffer fainting fits from lack of proper food and warm lodging. Feeling some desperation, she chose to reveal her identity to the regiment's sergeant, who arrested her. She was moved to a convent, interrogated as a spy, and eventually released, though she was required to sign an agreement not to tell or sell her story.

This put her in a different kind of a bind—unable to capitalize on her adventure. All the details of her tale she wrote in a book called *Sapper Dorothy Lawrence*[59] that was released only after the war. But the book got mediocre reviews and Lawrence continued to have a problem getting steady work. She seemed to suffer from some kind of post-traumatic stress.

She was institutionalized at Hanwell Lunatic Asylum in 1925 and was to spend nearly 40 years there before she died at the Friern Barnet Hospital in 1964, never gaining celebrity or renown for cycling to the WWI front and slipping into a regiment disguised as a male.

To Dorothy the bicycle was a tool, a means to an end. The military of Britain, Belgium, Germany, France, and Italy all used the bicycle as a mobility tool during the first World War, and so Dorothy was able to bicycle without undue notice. Bicycles let troops move quickly and they helped transport supplies. The U.S. didn't enter the war until 1917, but three companies produced nearly 30,000 American bicycles—a standard issue, fatigue-colored diamond frame—for the war. But once those soldiers came home, Henry Ford was gearing up to make a car that nearly all of them could afford.

CHAPTER SEVEN

Persisting Through a Changing World

(1920-1949)

Girton Girls and the Manhattan Five

Even after the Nineteenth Amendment was ratified in 1920, giving white women in the United States the right to vote, women were still expected to take the bulk of child rearing, not work out of the home unless economically pressed, and to learn from girlhood to subordinate themselves to men. For that brief period of around 1895 to 1900, bicycle-riding women likely felt that the freedom they experienced from cycling had the possibility of transforming the rest of their lives. But just as the right to vote had taken so much longer than activists thought when the suffrage movement began in the 1820s, the ideas of freedom and equality would take a long time to evolve into actual legal protections. The 1920s would prove to have some tantalizing tastes of freedom for women, but little strides forward in equality. Nothing gives that flavor quite like a photo of actors Buster Keaton and Sybil Seely together on a bicycle around 1922. In the publicity photo, Keaton's manning the pedals, looking like he's about to launch them on a great adventure. Meanwhile Seely is sitting precariously, perched between the handlebars—she's the bicycle ornament! He looks suspicious, she looks anxious, her shoulders crunched toward her ears, as if she's just waiting for the fall.

Of course, one picture doesn't paint an era—it's just one visual puzzle piece. What we do know is that in the 1920s women were not being aggressively marketed to by bicycle and motorcycle producers. They were an afterthought. In motorcycle marketing, women were viewed as sidecar riders, fine ornamentation to the man manning the motorcycle but hardly ever taking charge of the handlebars and throttle themselves. One of the highest cultural ideals in the 1910s and into the '20s for women was a life of service—to the family, her children and husband, and perhaps also her country—through selflessness.

University campuses may have offered an exception. Education was giving girls another set of ideas they might not have been getting in mainstream media and advertising. Girton College, now part of the University of Cambridge, was established as early as 1869 to give British women a place to get an education completely separate from men, so as to avoid any hint of impropriety between the sexes. Girton helped usher in an era of higher education for women, and Girton Girls were quickly stereotyped as bluestockings—bicycle riding, bloomer wearing, man hating, and uppity.

By the early 1920s, a troupe of Girton Girls toured the US as part of different vaudeville acts—the subtitle of their shows was "Tom-Boys on Wheels." These cycling college girls were a bicycle dance group not unlike the modern-day Sprockettes. They wore short mini-dresses and saucy hats while providing "Frills! Spills! Thrills!" to audiences from Muncie, Indiana to Salt Lake City, Utah, all the way through 1928. The Girton Girls continued a thread that runs through much of women's early biking: unable to be equally represented or have the same access as white male cyclists, these talented bicycle women resorted to tricks in music halls and vaudeville shows, dressed and cavorting just at the edge of polite society for the male gaze and for money. Though the performers were characterized as slightly daredevil, the act was more in the spirit of vaudeville and trading on the cache of being (supposedly) college-educated.

Between 1910 and 1930 the number of women attending college ballooned from about 140,000 before the start of the Great War to 480,000 by the start of the Great Depression. A photograph from Smith College in Massachusetts in 1929 shows the then-new Smith bicycle garage, with women—in fur scarves and long stockings—pulling their bikes into the racks, though inches of snow covered the ground. Another photo from the same era shows "Smithies" in elegant furs and pearls but posed smiling and proud with their books and their bikes.

Fewer women of color had the opportunity to go to college; about one in 1,000 African Americans gained college degrees during the time of the social and intellectual movement called the Harlem Renaissance in the 1920s. But fewer doesn't mean none. In the spring of 1928, a group of five young African-American women cyclists set out from Manhattan. They aimed their bicycles toward Washington, D.C. These young women were unknowns, and their Easter weekend jaunt 250 miles south to the nation's capitol wasn't a spur of the moment lark, nor was it to get a prize or win a bet. It was done, one of them told an inquiring newspaper, simply for a love of the outdoors and because they liked to bike. Historian Marya McQuertir discovered their story while researching her PhD thesis and was fascinated by the thought of the five young black women making a challenging bicycle journey over a long weekend.

The women, Leolya Nelson, Constance White, Mary Lou Jackson, Ethel Miller and Velva Jackson, dressed for the days-long trek in nearly-matching knickerbockers and sporty checked socks. McQuertir uncovered their general route—100+ miles to Philadelphia their first day, then a 50-mile day, and then again 100+ miles to reach their destination on the third day.

Leolya Nelson was likely their leader. A physical education instructor who had graduated from Syracuse University with a B.S. degree and gone on to Columbia for further education, she had run the fitness department of the Manhattan YWCA. The group spent the first night at the Philadelphia YWCA. Leolya told newspapers that bicycling was her favorite hobby. It is possible that all the five were members of the YWCA near their homes.

"The sole motive of the trip was the great out-of-doors as cherished by each of the riders," said the New York *The Age* newspaper. "They received a geographic disillusionment about "down South," reporting that they did more riding "up" than "down."[60]

The group went sightseeing at the Mall, took in the blossoming cherry trees, and caught the train back to New York. None went on to fame and fortune, from what McQuertir has uncovered, yet their strong cycling skills and fearless adventuring show a side of women's cycling few believe existed in the 1920s.

In the 1920s, a few flappers—freedom loving young women—also demanded the freedom to bike. The era's well-known actress Colleen Moore, who gained renown playing bobbed-hair flappers in the early years of her career, was an ardent bicyclist. In the 1920s flappers were assumed to be cutting their hair short, experimenting with smoking cigarettes and drinking gin, and spending the evenings in smoky clubs, dancing and carousing. Moore preferred riding her bike around movie sets.

But for the purposes of the media, the automobile was more the flapper's mobility machine. Zelda Fitzgerald, queen of the flappers, wore scandalously short pants and posed in front of an automobile on her honeymoon, similar to how young women of the 1890s posed proudly in their bloomer outfits after bike weddings of thirty years previously. Just as the bicycle was an incredible escape vehicle for the couples of the 1890s, who could ride away from the prying eyes of their parents, in the 1920s the automobile became the way to get away, especially for those with the economic means. But the bike still held some appeal as human-powered freedom and mobility. In later letters to Scott Fitzgerald, Zelda describes bicycling in a nostalgic and dreamlike manner, detailing rides she'd like to take in Guatemala down tree-lined, back country roads.[61]

In spite of the Girton Girls and other hints that girls and women may have been a viable market niche, the bicycle industry chose to firm up its commitment to boys in the

1920s, according to Robert Turpin in his book *First Taste of Freedom*. "In fact, the bicycle and Boy Scout were often promoted together as a means for instilling confidence, strength, and self-reliance in American boys," Turpin said.[62] Girls tended to be an afterthought, looking on attentively as a boy unwrapped his new bicycle or with admiration as he hopped on and zoomed away. And as the roaring '20s ended and the Great Depression began, women would continue bicycling but were pushed by the media and the Hollywood movie machine into a pinup role, playing to male desires with a combination of athletic appeal and scanty outfits.

Pinup

R acy photos of semi-nude women sitting on, standing next to, or even lying atop a bicycle were a staple of the late 1880s through the 1890s. What could be more titillating than a curvaceous woman, charmingly draped near or over that technological marvel, the bicycle? After all, if the bicycle helped regular women jettison pounds of underwear and throw off super-tight corsets, a bicycle as part of a racy shot that revealed even more female flesh seemed like something the New Woman should take in stride. But of course, the revelation of female flesh was mostly intended for the benefit of men and the protection or control of women.

Anna Held, the music hall performer who was the common-law wife of Florenz Zigfield and helped his troupe of dancers achieve national appeal, was one of the earliest bicycle pin-up girls. Held posed in a strapless ball gown with her body draped over a safety, in a soft focus shot from the early 1890s. The shot looks inspired by the series of bicycle advertisements, usually from French makers, that came around that time, showing buxom lovelies floating near bicycles in revealing diaphanous sheets. An ad for French Deesse bikes is one well-known example, and one for Cycles Sirius is another.

Anna had a classic hour-glass figure and Zigfield, a master of media manipulation, cashed in. He told the press tall tales about Anna and her bicycle prowess, including one involving her saving a judge from a runaway horse by quick thinking while she was bicycle riding—this was told before Held had actually been riding a bike. Anna used the bicycle as a prop throughout her career and even had a cycling "suit" she helped design that was sold by the Jordan, Marsh department stores.

According to art history professor Maria Elena Buszek, the pin-up was born in the 19th century as a photographic calling card by theatrical and entertainment women who used it like social media. It worked for bicycle racer Tillie Anderson. Tillie made a real effort to appear more attractive in her photographic calling cards, perhaps because the press seemed to think she wasn't a beauty.

Tillie and her competitors wore athletic gear that may have titillated some fans.

Filmy semi-nudes floating on or near a bicycle were a staple of bicycle advertising that took a brief hiatus in the teens and the WWI era. Bicycle ads in *Motorcycle Illustrated* were more likely to touch a chord of patriotism than sex appeal. With the advent of the cultural popularity of going to the movies, the bicycle regained favor as a pinup backdrop.

A few bicycle manufacturers that hung on through the 1920s finally went bust at the start of the Depression. In one of its cyclical resurgences, the bicycle market started to improve around 1932, and adults buying bicycles for transportation were said to be causing part of the uptick. It's interesting that bike historians don't talk much about this period—it was another real chance for the bike to become an equal in the transport mix. In 1934 bike sales were the best they had been in ten years, and by 1936 it was nothing less than a banner year, with 1.2 million bicycles manufactured. Ignaz Schwinn closed his motorcycle factory but kept his bicycle line going, introducing the first "balloon tires" in 1933. Newspaper pundits heralded the amazing two-wheeled revival, and even tandems made a comeback.

It seemed like the economy and an interest in health, PR, and pretty women all contributed to this upswing. The cycling industry did a campaign to make biking seem health-promoting, while the Hollywood PR machines were also in full swing, cranking out publicity stills of stars by the gazillions. Putting a starlet onto a bicycle was a sure-fire way to make her seem wholesome and sexy at the same time. In 1930, a starlet named Nancy Carroll was pictured in a Peter Pan hat and somewhat risqué trousers riding solo on a tandem bike as she relaxed with her family (or so the caption says… the "family" is not shown in the photo) in Phoenix, Arizona. By 1932, a small group of reported stars and starlets were biking for pleasure. The newspapers claimed that a power couple, actress Jobyna Ralston and actor Richard Arlen, were part of the bicycling trend, as well as starlets Dorothy Lee and Leila Hyams. A former bicycle racer named Hans Ohrt helped things along by establishing a popular bike store in Beverly Hills in 1937. Later, Ohrt took groups of happy cyclists—he himself rode a tandem or three-seater bike with his wife and another rider—along the wide boulevards of Beverly Hills. It was an early version of present-day tours of the mansions of the Hollywood stars.

It is the photographs of women bicycle riding in the 1930s that surprise with their depiction of what was considered healthy, wholesome, and sexy, and which likely went far in getting a new generation of adults onto their bikes. Importantly, Hollywood stars had the ability and the means to frequently vacation (which a big swatch of America at that time did not). And where did these elites go? Many of them went to Bermuda, an island paradise that at that time banned motorized vehicles. Bicycles swarmed on the streets alongside horse-drawn carriages. The photo ops in this warm winter escape abounded. Even closer to home was Palm Springs, the perfect place for paparazzi to catch beautiful people posing on bikes.

Pictures of starlet-to-star Mary Pickford on a bicycle set off the new era of bike pinup photos. Warner Brothers, Paramount, and MGM were all adept at these silly, sexy bike photos, that ranged from a quartet of female bike polo players in 1932 (shades of the Girton Girls) to a woman named Maxine Cantrell supposedly shopping for bike tires in high heels and short shorts, to starlet Grace Bradley in a sort-of bathing suit sitting atop an obviously stationary high wheel antique. There is even a shot of Judy Garland, adorably young in a polka-dot ensemble, checking her bike tires for air; one of Margaret Sullivan eating an apple and holding a tennis racket next to a bike; and one of Ginger Rogers riding a man's bike quite gracefully.

Some of the photos are staged and sweet, like Shirley Temple wearing curlers on a bike. Others are clearly ridiculous, like Gary Cooper on a tandem with Fay Wray, whose trailing filmy confection of a dress would surely get tangled in the chain after a single pedal revolution.

By the 1930s the safety of bicycling was in jeopardy as cars became more numerous, speeding ever more rapidly along the country's lanes and roads. Yet while this meant in the United States the bicycle was no longer preeminent for transportation, it still held people's attention for recreation. And it was a potent symbol of youthfulness, freedom, and joy, thus a great and useful prop for pinups.

Unfortunately, a lot of those photos treated the women models as nothing more than visual ornamentation.

In any case by 1938, a good year for bike sales was also a peak year for pure cheesecake bike photos with the arrival of starlet Betty Grable on the scene. Grable's legs were considered the ultimate in siren sexiness: long, smooth, and literally insured for a million bucks! A shot from 1938 is classic BG pin-up—Betty stands with her back (and those gams) to the camera, in shorts and a halter top, holding a man's bike in front of her. The photo is publicity for the movie "College Swing" and was the first of many photos of Grable biking. While she had a long fruitful career as an actress, it was her legs, and those pin ups, that made her famous. And Grable (and the bike) were about to get an added boost from the next World War just around the corner.

Victory Bike

When the U.S. finally engaged in WWII after Pearl Harbor, there was a rush of propaganda that highlighted patriotic practices—there were Victory gardens, and there were also Victory bicycles. A first prototype ordered by the government was made by the Huffman Manufacturing Co., and it looked very much like modern-day cargo delivery bikes, with a large basket in front, a slightly smaller front wheel, and a sturdy kickstand. An iconic bicycle photo of the prototype and the early war period is the one in which Len Henderson of the Office of Price Administration took his secretary-stenographer out for a ride on a Victory bike, reproducing that thoroughly dated and overdone—but obviously effective—meme of woman as bicycle ornament in the front basket or between the handlebars. Leon Henderson was the cigar-chomping bureaucrat maneuvering the pared down, war-time cargo bike, with Betty Barrett as the pinup cutie, her saddle-shoed feet spilling over the bike's basket top. The bicycle pinup in new and patriotic format was alive and well.

The Victory bike itself was a result of the push-pull between America's necessity for local transport and the need to implement rationing. Automobile tires were quickly rationed in 1942 after Pearl Harbour—a single car tire of that time took 16 pounds of rubber and much of the raw product was in countries controlled by Japanese forces—so the U.S. decided to give thrifty cargo cycling by adults a nod.

Bicycles themselves were also being rationed. The Office of Production Management looked at the prototype for the Victory bicycle and then specified that all bikes manufactured in the U.S. must be lightweight—no more than 31 pounds, and without the balloon tires then in vogue, or other fripperies. Under the rationing, only two models of bicycle could be made, one for women, one for men. Kids' models disappeared completely in this short war era! Production of these was set at 750,000[63]—far fewer bicycles than pre-war production—but as the Smithsonian notes, more *adult* bicycles than the years prior. Manufacturing of all other bicycles was halted in the U.S.

Amazingly, after a couple of decades of child-oriented marketing, the authorities expected adults to suddenly take up the bike even though there was the limit on production and no grand campaign to sell the bike on its merits. "Investigation indicates," says the *New York Times* in 1942, "that travel to market by bicycle will increase rather than diminish." Propaganda alert! Housewives were supposedly going to bike more and do their patriotic duty, wearing out bike tires instead of automobile tires. But this article gave no stats to indicate that bicycling actually was rising. The *Times* went on to say that Mrs. Franklin D. Roosevelt had bought a bike, though the article reported that she hadn't learned to ride it. (That seems in error, as there's an early photograph of Eleanor with a bike at around age 10 in various biographies.)

The article, somewhat bombastically, also claimed women weren't seeing an increase in suitable sportswear for bike riding, leading them to "makeshift ensembles, often unsuitable." Some things don't change, at least not by this time. For bicycle riding the author, thankfully unknown, recommended women wear a "jupe-culotte" (basically a shin-length divided skirt) with a leather jacket and a "hood tied securely under the chin."[64] Cycle chic, indeed.

A 1943 Aetna Life Insurance Company short film reinforced the idea that women were enthusiastically riding bikes for the war effort. "Before the war," the voiceover says, "bicycles are used principally for recreation and pleasure." But now, the bicycle was going to play a vital part in "relieving America's transportation problems." Wow! Boys and girls would cycle to school, men and women would "pedal smoothly and conveniently" to their jobs and families would use the bike for all their errands. Bicycle paradise.

There was a hitch. Those damned automobiles. The Warrenton, Missouri *Banner* commented in February of 1942, "With sugar rationing and seeing so many pleasingly plump ladies bicycling, we are all expecting to see a nation of unusually willowly [sic] women gracing the landscapes soon."[65] At the same time there wasn't a push for bicycle infrastructure or safety for riders. Many of the articles about biking early in the war, like the *New York Times*, were admonishing rather than realistic and encouraging. For example, John Wallace, a safety director in the police department of Mason City, Iowa, told a Girl Scout troop in the city in 1943 that bicycling had tripled over the six previous years. He said that bicycling was "difficult," more difficult than driving a car, but that it was a necessary form of transportation during the war. Wallace noted that 7,000 people were killed on their bicycles, and 34,000 injured over the previous year. What a way to encourage these young Scouts to go for their cycling "badges"![66]

Wallace was highlighting something that was beginning to sink in with people—the exponential uptake of the auto was overall making biking much less safe for cyclists. Statisticians from the Metropolitan Life Insurance Company reported in the health workers' magazine *Hygeia* that in 1933 there were approximately 400 deaths from bike-car collisions. By 1941—right before the wartime restrictions on driving—the U.S. bike fatalities rose to over 900. (This statistic puts Wallace's 7,000 figure to some doubt.) The largest part of the deaths, said the statisticians, was amongst boys aged 10 to 19.[67]

An article by Mary E. Bostwick in the *Indianapolis Star* quoted a sporting-goods retailer, H.H. Behrent, who said: "if it could be arranged to provide bicycle lanes on the street—lanes three, four feet wide, next to the curb—bicyclists would emerge from hiding like angleworms after a rain. As it is, traffic doesn't give a person on a bike a chance."[68] Bostwick noted that the 1942 Schwinn bicycle catalog painted some very pretty pictures of young people biking, but failed to put a single car in the illustrations. Bostwick also pointed out that many people who purchased bicycles in that early war period expected that tire rationing would cause a lot less driving, but that that hadn't necessarily occurred (yet) in Indianapolis, at least not enough to get the cyclists out in droves.

By the following year ongoing automobile gas rationing caused the government's Office of Price Administration to increase its bike quotas, and to also allow adults with jobs to purchase bikes for transportation purposes. Americans were finally beginning to feel the full brunt of wartime restrictions. Bicycling blossomed. According to Aetna Life's 1943 film *Points for Pedalers*, there were by mid 1943 more than 12,000,000 people bicycling in the U.S.[69] Though the armed forces had taken the lion's share of newly-produced bikes, companies involved in the war effort (and there were many) were forming bicycle brigades—groups of cyclists riding to work together. Some companies even provided bike parking infrastructure for their employees. What was fascinating is that in this relatively condensed period of time, the United States started to experience all the pros and cons of a ramp-up in cycling. Looking through the newspaper record it's clear to see that some of the problems (people riding bikes on sidewalks, more injuries and collisions with cars) were the same as we experience today in urban environments. But also some of the same prospective positive effects are mentioned, such as improved health and weight loss. And one of the best additional effects for women was that the era of wearing pants, slacks, and jeans was (finally) being securely ushered in.

To our modern eye the bloomer suits of the 1890s seem practical yet visually outlandish. And when looking at the many photographs of the era, it seems the body-hugging fit and the cinching at both waist and shins of the bloomer suit made it less readily accepted. It wasn't generous or adaptable enough to enjoy universal popularity with U.S. women. Many women who took to the bike during the initial eras stuck with a skirt, sometimes divided, for their cycling. Young women like Kittie Knox had the figure and the daring, and thus were the main consumers of bloomer suits. But bloomer suits faded to obscurity at the beginning of the twentieth century.

Prior to WWI, women were also still wearing corsets, though less constricting ones, and were culturally expected to be demure, modest, and almost always, dressed in a skirt. They were also expected to wear a hat and gloves when out and about. When the U.S. finally did enter the "Great War," women were able to get some societal leeway to wear pants in certain situations. Some of the volunteer units of the American Red Cross allowed a few women to put on knickerbockers/breeches, bloomers beneath a skirt, or actual trousers, usually under a long coat or smock.

Working women who had rough or dirty jobs or who were handling heavy equipment might get a uniform of pants via a coverall. When WWI ended, though dress fashions had become more liberal, and Coco Chanel helped bring in the era of the dropped waist dress (i.e. specifically sans corset), pants for women were again sidelined to very specific occasions. Teen school girls could dress up in outfits of oxfords, knickers, and men's shirts and ties. At certain sports such as golf, women were allowed to wear loose floppy knickers and vests. Fashionable flappers also had the leeway to put on flowy pajama outfits with matching tops and pants in silky materials, as beachwear. But for cycling in the teens and twenties, it was mostly still a skirt world.

By the early '30s, though, and coinciding with the bicycle pinup, fashion deemed that a kind of pantsuit was suitable for women to cycle in. The wide pant legs of the bottom half of the suit were made from a soft and draped material, and pleated, so that off the bike they gave the effect of a skirt. Elsa Schiaparelli helped make them famous, and acceptable. "Neat pyjama costumes," said the *Sunday Avalanche Journal*, "'[are] the new mode when milady pedals forth to scorch the pavement."[70] By 1933, divided skirts, slacks, and even shorts were seen on the fashion pages. Bicycle "frocks" in polka-dotted pique could do double duty for tennis and beach wear, according to the fashion pundits. And shorts! They weren't the short shorts of today, and again they were a new item mainly seen on very young, thin, and daring women. But the Hollywood pinup had brought the short into circulation, and no better place to wear it than on the bike.

At first that was actually about the only place you were supposed to wear them, or on the tennis court. Paired with a jaunty little skull cap or beret, a sporty woman could put on her shorts and take a ride. A sporty woman. For the majority, day dresses in the 1930s still came down to mid-calf and were fairly demure. Slacks for daywear were considered pushing the envelope even for a star as bright as Katharine Hepburn.

The Great Kate

Katherine Hepburn was a headstrong actress and leading Hollywood star by the late 1930s, and as her stardom grew she practically single handedly took on the establishment's dislike of pants on women. She had a steadfast love of both jeans and tailored slacks. There's an apocryphal story of Hepburn coming out of her trailer in the mid-1930s in her underwear and refusing to go on with shooting (or get dressed) until jeans that had been purloined from her dressing room were returned to her.

If ever there was a multipurpose heroine for city cyclists and their wardrobes, it was Katharine Hepburn. Born near Hartford, Connecticut, in 1907, she was one of the few Hollywood starlets shown in bike glamour shots of the 1930s and 1940s who actually enjoyed a steady, joyful, and long term cycling habit.

Hepburn was an early bicyclist due to Hartford's renown as a bicycling mecca, and also because of her strong-willed father. He had a custom diamond-frame bike built for her when she was just three years old, at Hartford's Pope Manufacturing Company. It was 1910, and Hepburn's dad taught her to ride via the sink-or-swim method: he simply balanced her on top of the saddle and pushed her down a hill. Careening down to the bottom, Hepburn crashed into a pedestrian and was thrown unharmed to the grass. She said she fell in love with bicycling from that day forward.

She rode all over the city on her bike, never hindered by her mother telling this tomboy to be ladylike. According to Hepburn, she and her brother Tom raced the trolley cars on Farmington Avenue for fun, and she always claimed to like cycling better than horse riding for the measure of control and fun it gave her.

The publicity shots with movie stars on bicycles that were particularly popular in the late 1930s all the way through the 1950s included plenty of Kate on bikes. Fellow actor Theodore Bikel said she was the only superstar that regularly rode her bicycle around the Warner Brothers lot. In fact, Hepburn enjoyed cycling nearly everywhere she went. On many of her movie shoots on location, her pattern seemed to be: work all day, take a bike ride in the afternoon or evening, and retire early. Later in life, she could be seen in slacks and a shirt and sweater, cycling undaunted through Manhattan traffic.

Hepburn rode well into her later years. At the age of 72, playing Lily Moffat in a television production of *The Corn Is Green*, Hepburn experienced what early women cyclists must have often felt. Dressed in a long skirt and lots of undergarments and riding a heavy 1890s-style upright bike, she tried again and again to make it up a hill without wobbling. Eventually, Hepburn had to reluctantly relinquish the scene to a stunt double.

Kate obviously had access to tailors; her pants were always skillfully fitted to her frame. Other women weren't so fortunate, as manufacturers took a while to jump into ready-made pants for women. At first the styles were quite high-waisted, with extra large cuffs not suitable for biking. The fashion writers of this early phase of the war in the 1940s seemed to have forgotten or never knew that cycling was popular in the 1930s, commenting that "for the first time since the turn of the century and the "bloomer girls," America is seeing distinct bicycle fashions."[71] What?

It seems more true to say that for the first time since the 1890s the media and the war machine were paying attention to women cyclists' need for practical bike fashions. Designer Charles Armour put forth a "town bicycle suit" with a tailored jacket and rather strange pants with wide culotte legs and big pleats that made them in essence just another version of the divided skirt. The outfit included a little hat somewhat reminiscent of Miss Gulch's spinster millinery in the *Wizard of Oz*.

In the mainstream, as more and more women did jobs that made slacks practical, the variety of ready-mades got better. Trousers with ankle buttons appeared to help keep the cuff cloth out of the crank and chain. In addition, trouser clips and clamps were popular, as were pants sharply tapered at the ankle. And while the term "pedal pusher" came about in the late 1860s to describe people who bike, in 1942 it began to appear as an actual item of clothing specifically for female bicyclists. Also called long shorts or short pants, pedal pushers described an exact length, falling precisely just past the knee. But though the bicycle gave rise to the pedal pusher, in just a few short years the terminology and the style itself split away from the bike, so that "pedal pusher" could signify an old-time bicycle racer or the pants.

Pants for women, whether short or long, were a staple, and though post-war they again took a backseat to a girdled, dirndl style of dresses for women, they would never again be quite as stigmatized an article of clothing as they once were. Katherine Hepburn was partially responsible for this shift. In her later years she used the bicycle to stay active, and died at age 96 in 2003.

Evelyn Hamilton

Born in London 1906, Eveline Alice Alexandra Bayliss preferred to be called Evelyn. She reportedly married John Hamilton in 1926 and the pair rode a tandem together around the English countryside. She was too late for the zenith of early women's bicycle racing. But her strength and endurance on the bicycle could not be dampened, and by 1931 Evelyn won both the first women's British National Half-Mile Handicap race, and in that same year, the Sporting Life Trophy. She quickly befriended one of the country's master bike frame builders, Claud Butler, and Butler sponsored her in 1934 when she attempted an endurance ride of 1,000 miles in 7 days. Britain proclaimed

Hamilton's attempt was the first time a Brit and the first time a woman had tried the feat; however, we know Elsa von Blumen accomplished it back in 1882, and Margaret Gast in 1900 did 1,000 miles in 99 hours.

But the institutional memory of the press can be short, and Evelyn Hamilton did shave some hours off Margaret Gast's feat by getting the 1,000 miles done in 84 hours. To celebrate, Claud Butler produced a commemorative bicycle frame similar to the one Evelyn used and called it the "Miss Modern" a rather unfortunate though alliterative moniker for a new fast racing bike specifically designed for a female frame.

Evelyn was ambitious. On the 14th of August, 1934 she set out to do 10,000 miles over 100 days of riding. Her Granby bike (for some reason she by this time had eschewed the Claud Butler frame) had the latest in gearing technology, similar to the derailleurs of our era. Hamilton received quite a bit of media coverage for her ride and was featured in a number of British Pathé films about cycling, even riding a comfy recumbent bike in one clip. As the war intensified, Hamilton's path grew strange and a bit mysterious; perhaps current bicycle historians will begin to tease the real truth out of some of the tall tales about this British cyclist's life and exploits. Some accounts have Hamilton sneaking off to France, perhaps to ride with a circus and perform in a "wall of death" similar to the one that killed Dottie Farnsworth decades earlier. Evelyn's story was that she got trapped in Paris after the start of the Nazi occupation of that city.

By the time the war was over, Evelyn had taken the name Helsen. In later interviews she said she had lived together with Fernand Maurice Helsen, who was also married. She claimed she assumed the identity of a dead woman because she was on a Nazi wanted list. What happened to her first husband isn't (yet) known. What is known is that in 1938 Evelyn had opened a bicycle shop in Streatham, London which stayed open during the years of WWII. Eventually she returned to London, and it appeared Helsen died in Streatham in 1950. Evelyn Hamilton was awarded the Cross of Lorraine as part of the Médaille de la Résistance Française by De Gaulle in 1943, and many accounts claim she worked as part of the Free French Forces, in resistance against the occupation.

Evelyn used the design of the Cross of Lorraine as a bicycle badge and produced a very limited line of bikes. She lived to be 99, died in 2005 and was buried with a gravestone giving her name as Evelyn Alice Helsen.

CHAPTER EIGHT

Girdled (1950-Today)

Mouseketeers

At the end of WWII and with the start of the 1950s, American women were expected (and directed in advertising) to take their coveralls off and put their aprons back on, over new-fangled, shorter crinolines and in many cases, an inner layer of constricting girdle. The corset was gone but the girdle got great endorsement. Girls still biked, and if they were youth or teens were allowed fashion freedom. But in the mainstream, women were squeezed, forced, or chose to embrace a new domesticity which included girdles, dirndls, and poodle skirts. Also required was pointy, breast-lifting bras and lots of personal beautification, whether they wanted these things—and many probably did—or whether they didn't. Some women hated giving up the exhilaration of working, earning, and being free. But the culture, through mainstream advertising, dictated no more Rosie the Riveter head scarfs, at least not in public. And forget biking back and forth to work when you could and should use your shiny new automobile instead!

Of course the picture painted by advertisers was far from the entire story of the breadth of women's experience and situation. But certain advances in different industries and in consumer culture in general left bicycling for adults once more in the slow lane. Except! The decade of the '50s seemed a period in which there was always a headline here and there of outlier women on bikes doing long bike tours or treks. Likely there were plenty of young men taking similar treks, but they weren't considered as newsworthy for the male-dominant media. Fresh-faced young (white) girls doing the same trips were slow-day catnip to newspaper people.

One thing that aided young women in making solo long-distance bike tours was the springing up of hostels across the U.S. Biking from hostel to hostel as a solo white woman was relatively easy in 1950. Not immensely popular, but not impossible. The Bicycle Institute of America (the former

PR arm of the bike manufacturers' trade organization) enthused in 1950 that a million Americans had taken up biking in the year previous, while they proclaimed that a Dr. Nathan E. Cohen had published a book called *Bike Ways* in which he said the bike is "a unifying force in American life."[72] This was Dr. Cohen's wishful thinking. It was clearly the auto that was a unifying and at the same time an alienating force in American life.

It's not clear to this author whether women in the 1950s lived in a dream or a nightmare—possibly it was both, simultaneously. Because of the availability of a sudden surge of consumer products, American women had access to a slew of new beauty aids: cosmetics and face creams, lingerie and ready-made affordable outfits, time saving appliances and fancy stuff, stuff, stuff. At the same time that economic forces and globalization were making American families richer and giving them a better quality of life (and of course this was more possible for white Americans than for other groups), women were expected to be virgins and sex bombs at the same exact time.

Could anything be more confusing? Take the case of Anette Funicello, known to early Boomer kids as the Mouseketeer par excellence. Funicello also happened to win the title Bicycle Queen of 1959, bestowed upon her by the Bicycle Institute of America (BIA). Her win of this rather empty tribute capped, in retrospect, a weird decade for women cyclists. The BIA and also the League of American Wheelmen had sponsored a "Bicycle Queen" pageant during the 1950s at fairs and bike events, crowning a comely and well-dressed (but completely conventional) woman as queen. Funicello won the honor in 1959, and the promotional picture of her showcases the iconography of the time. There's Anette, at 16 years old, straddling a clunky cruiser bike with balloon tires, no gears, and no hand brakes. Built to go slow. Anette was a pretty, fresh-faced teenager, though also carefully coiffed and groomed, breasts pinched into a pointy bra and hips squeezed into tight pedal pushers, her beauty-queen sash draped over her chest. It was hard to believe she was actually going to ride the bike at all.

Nancy Neiman and Doris Travani

As Peter Nye documents in his book *Hearts of Lions: The History of American Bicycle Racing*, the second era of bicycle racing for women emerged in the 1950s. Girls could join cycling clubs and participate in amateur races–professional teams did not exist for women in the US.

Nancy Neiman was born in Detroit in 1933 and started bicycle touring in 1950; she was part of the group of cyclists who used the strong American Youth Hostel network of places to stay while they rode. Fairly quickly, Neiman turned to bike racing. She hadn't been allowed to have a bicycle until she graduated from grade school. Working as a Detroit secretary, she trained with a coach named Gene Portuesi and competed in her spare time against the dismay of her mother, who thought racing unladylike.

Nancy had a strong will and competitive drive, and women's racing was getting more attention, with plenty of talented British and French female cyclists already racing. In 1956, at the height of her career, Nancy toured Europe and competed in stage races. There's an awesome photo of her getting an impromptu leg massage by Evelyn Hamilton while she was in Britain. She won the American national bicycle championship four times: in 1953, 1954, 1956, and 1957. Her career spanned seven years from 1952-1958. After her marriage, Nancy Neiman Baranet wrote a memoir of her 1956 racing experience, *The Turned Down Bar*.

Doris Travani and Nancy Neiman were both natives of Detroit, though Doris grew up in a racing family and thus started to bike at a much earlier age. Born in 1929, Travani was just 12 years old when she began racing—her father was the national bicycling champion of Italy in 1920, and her brother Bob was also a racing cyclist. She raced for the Wolverine Sports Club, which turned out quite a few winning cyclists. By 1946, Doris won her first amateur title, and followed that with first-place wins in 1948, 1949, and 1950. Her brother competed in the 1948 Olympics, but women cyclists were not allowed to compete in the Olympic games until 1984. After 10 years of competitive racing, Doris married and raised a family, as did Neiman

Baranet. They were both inducted into the US Bicycling Hall of Fame, Nancy Neiman Baranet in 1992, and Doris Travani Mulligan in 2013.

Pedal Pushing

The year 1960 might have been America's best as far as prosperity, global hegemony, and self satisfaction. For the first time in the country's history, its citizens had as much leisure time as they had work time, according to the National Recreation Association. Over 2,200 hours per year were available to a family of four for leisure activities, and thus American families eagerly bought lots of stuff to enjoy their hobbies. Half a million outdoor swimming pools were installed in 1960, and sports enthusiasts spent $35 billion on equipment. Boating, not biking, was the top family "sport," yet bicycling retailers claimed that family biking was at a new peak of popularity, with the PRish

Bicycle Institute of America (BIA) saying that family biking was almost as popular as "during the gay '90s." Hunting and fishing were considered the top solo leisure activities, while golf was gaining ground as a man's (especially a business man's) preferred outdoor leisure.

BIA also said at that time that 27 million bicycles were out on the roads and that nearly 5 million college students depended on the bike to get to and from campuses across the country. Vassar and Radcliffe women were noted to be particularly devoted to their bikes. Banana-seat bicycles like Schwinn Sting-Rays—dubbed "high rise" bikes—became highly valued by the younger set. But the bad news? By 1960, 59 million passenger cars were plying the roads, and Chrysler then-president Tex Colbert joked that the compact car was designed to lure even more bike riders away from their two wheels. In Robert Turpin's view, 1960 marks the moment at which the change in bicycle marketing from adults to children was complete. By that time, 80% of American homes had at least one car, and 15% had a second auto. Thus 80% of bikes sold went to youth, primarily boys.

The BIA, somewhat naively, said that the bicycle's benefits were just so outstanding that bikes could stand up to rampant automobility. Cyclists, BIA said, had figured out that bicycling was an inexpensive form of transportation *and* recreation that would help them "enjoy their spare time–a means of improving their physical condition."[73]

Paul Dudley White, President Eisenhower's physician, endorsed biking, and in 1962 he dedicated the first U.S. "Bikeway" in Homestead, Florida (ironically, as Florida would gradually become the most deadly place for bicyclists!). Celebrity female bicyclists at the start of this era were Marilyn Monroe, Kim Novak, Shirley MacLaine and June Alyson. But women bicycling wasn't a part of popular cultural or even sporting norms. At the 1960 summer Olympics there were only two road cycling events and four track cycling events, all for men only, and it would be 24 more years before women's cycling events were introduced. The Tour de France, won in 1960 by Gastone Nancini, only allowed men. (Italian Alfonsina Strada, the first competitive staged-race cyclist, did the similar Giro d'Italia in 1924 but registered as "Alfonsin" to participate.)

In the Schwinn 1960 catalog, the sleekest-looking and most technologically up-to-date bike model, the 10-speed Continental, was advertised as available in men's models only, in 19, 21, and 23 inch frames. For women the models were called "Fair Lady," "Co-ed," "Starlet," "Debutante," and "Hollywood." There was also, thankfully, a dropped frame "Spitfire" and a "Tornado" for women.

It's important to note that from the long view, cycling didn't actually decline in the 1960s. Instead, bicycle sales rose slowly, perennially popular as gifts to children during Christmas—holiday sales constituted 30% or more of annual sales. The Bicycle Institute of America kept promoting family cycling, and was pleased by the steady sales increases. The pedal-pushing grandmas of Sarasota were a group of mobile-home women who formed a club to bike together each week, and coverage of their rides accentuated the fact that nobody was ever too old to ride a bike. Eisenhower's Dr. Dudley kept biking and promoted biking through the Kennedy era. And in New York City, a 1966 (weekend) ban on cars in Central Park drew adults on bicycles eager to escape the increasing pressures of urban life.

Then in the late 1960s, European and Japanese lightweight bicycles with derailleurs and ten gears began to appear in the United States, though they had been around in Europe at least a decade. The so-called 10-speed was a sensation, with dropped handlebars that racers had been using for decades but that were new to the more recreation-oriented bicycling crowd.

By 1970, the BIA reported bike sales growing at 30%. Another bike boom was on. Ecological and health concerns contributed—the first Earth Day was April 22, 1970. Schwinn, founded in 1885, had its biggest year in 1971 when it manufactured 1.25 million bikes. One New Jersey dealer told the local *Central New Jersey Home News* that it was housewives driving demand. "They're getting the old man out even though he doesn't want to go," said Joe Miczak of the Edison Cycle Shop.[74] By 1973, the energy crisis also fueled this latest boom.

Of course, in the twentieth century a boom always boomerangs, bringing to heart bike vs. car safety concerns.

Marie Birnbaum, a daily cyclist who worked at the Department of Transportation noted in 1973 that: "The bicycle is a very practical vehicle but it isn't a very safe one at the moment. No matter whose statistics you look at the picture is pretty bad."[75] Injuries and deaths increased nationwide. The blame fell mostly on the cyclists, who were accused of not having sufficient training, not acting in predictable ways, and not putting enough reflectors or lights on their bicycles. They were not accused of not wearing their helmets, because helmet wearing hadn't yet come to be seen as the requirement it now is.

This safety problem was recognized by officials, but the car was always given precedence. No one considered that bicycles and public transport could substitute for automobiles in the transport landscape. In fact, the quick rise of biking, and especially commuter and casual bicycling, was considered by some to hold the seeds of its own demise: John E. Hirten, an assistant to the secretary of transportation, held a conference that questioned whether the bicycle was a legitimate part of multi-modal urban transport. He concluded: "As bicyclists and bicycle enthusiasts, we find ourselves in a very difficult situation. In a way, success may be going to our head. The danger is that the bike may turn into the hoola hoop of the '70s."[76]

Warning signs about another bust began to sound in late 1974. The market softened and a wave of new regulations began to come into force that were meant to increase safety yet also increased prices. Thus, another boom went bust, and in 1976 sales were reported down by 50%. It wasn't until the 1980 hit movie *Breaking Away* that U.S. recreational cycling received a bit of a revival.

Blasting forward to the present, we are still on that same road in the U.S. that the "70s started to build; that slow, painful path of legitimizing bicycling in the face of massive automobility. Women bicyclists have certainly rolled the boulder forward over lots of little ups and downs. Many extraordinarily talented bicyclists have experienced triumphs, yet as a society and a culture, we've also experienced the never-ending tragedy of people dying on their bikes from collisions with cars due to lack of safer infrastructure. For women, gaining some kind of parity in all the different types of bicycling is still a series of uphills on a mountain where we cannot see the peak. The U.S. is such a vast country that good things in biking can be happening at the same time that terrible things are happening in biking.

CONCLUSION

I t is still somewhat hard to realize it, but men's bicycle racing in the 1880s through the 1920s was an exciting spectator sport in America, experiencing levels of popularity now reserved for football, baseball, and basketball. Women tried to participate in the early quest for speed and endurance, and in a scrabble to become legitimate, paid racing professionals. American bicycle racing was principally and primarily a man's sport, and even more so after the League contributed to killing women's racing in the late 1890s.

That makes the revival of women in competitive cycling starting around the 1950s all the more sweet and impressive.

As I hope this narrative shows, women started bicycling when men did, in spite of the clothing and cultural hurdles, and continued to bicycle in all the arenas that men did, though with many more hindrances and social pressures, and with less support than men.

Nancy Neiman Baranet and Doris Travani Mulligan and a few dozen other women joined mostly-male bicycle clubs, got encouragement from brothers or fathers, and gradually paved the way. As Nancy Neiman Baranet has said: "When I started, national championship divisions were men's open, juniors, which referred to boys fourteen to sixteen, and the "girls" division. I said, "Enough of this." When I won the national "girls" championship for the second time in 1954, I told ABL officials I was twenty-one and was no longer a girl. I said I wanted the name of the division switched to women's, and it was."[77]

Neiman retired from the racing circuit after her fourth win, and it was not until 1958, after she retired, that U.S. women cyclists were included in yearly world championships. Around that time, Audrey Phleger McElmury was an avid teen surfer and skateboarder in La Jolla, California. Born in Massachusetts in 1943, she started to bicycle when she broke her leg in a skateboarding crash, and in 1964 she won a women's cycling championship in California in track racing. She preferred road racing, which at that moment was exclusive to men, according to Peter Nye's *Hearts of Lions*.[78] She trained hard with men and put up with the harassment of being the only woman in any training group. In 1969, Audrey traveled to Czechoslovakia to compete at the world championship road race, and though she traveled with a team of three other women and eight men, the team was unable to fund her trip. After a gnarly 43-mile race in which she was ahead of the pack, she crashed on a downhill but was able to recover, managing to not only catch up with the pack but also to win, one minute and ten seconds ahead of the next finisher.

This made McElmury the first American, man or woman, to win that Road World Championship and don the winner's famed rainbow jersey. The newspapers called her "the new queen of cycling." Unfortunately, the interest in competitive road racing was much higher in Europe than in the U.S. With all the hurdles U.S. women have faced—lack of money, strong training clubs and support teams, and opportunity—it is amazing that a group of strong and competitive American women were inspired to follow on McElmury's fast-turning wheels. The United States Bicycling Hall of Fame in Davis, California, includes a lengthy list of women, most of whom garnered their achievements in some kind of bicycle competition. Thirty of the 158 inductees (18%) are women, coming from all areas of bicycling.

The challenges that plagued women cyclists from the very start of bicycling—gaining recognition and important measures of equality—are still with us. Women are still restricted in their ability to bicycle by cultural ideas of how we should and shouldn't do it, and what we should wear or look like while we're doing it. The gender gap in bicycling has of course narrowed, with the list of Hall of Fame inductees showing that women have everything needed to be every kind of winning bicyclist imaginable. There are plenty of role models, though not always of such fame as with male racing.

When multi-talented Frenchwoman Marie Marvingt was told she wasn't allowed to do the Tour de France in 1908 she did it anyway, one day behind the rest of the riders, and her times were better than many of the male riders. When Alfonsina Strada showed in 1924 that she could suffer the pain of the Giro d'Italia and keep on riding, she caused such a stir that the Giro made sure to keep her out the following year. And when American Marianne Martin won the first Tour de France Feminin in 1984 and received a mountain of positive press, ride officials still said the womens' racing competition didn't have the needed funding or support to stay alive. The fact that women can't participate in the regular Tour de France; that their own "Feminin" was killed; that women racers have a difficult time financially for the most part and that pay parity is pathetic, and that as recently as 2011 UCI president Pat McQuaid could with a straight face say that women's cycling hadn't developed enough for women to be paid a minimum wage for their work—all indicate how far we still may have to go. The thirteen amateur female cyclists who completed the Tour in 2018, following the same route as Marie Marvingt did in 1908, want the same thing Marvingt did and the same thing women bicyclists have wanted since the advent of the bicycle—that is, recognition, respect, and above all, an ongoing opportunity to ride.

The end.

U.S. BICYCLING HALL OF FAME WOMEN

Alison Dunlap • Audrey McElmury • Barbara George • Beth Heiden • Cheri Elliott • Connie Carpenter-Phinney • Connie Paraskevin • Doris Kopsky Muller • Doris Travani-Mulligan • Dottie Daling • Inga Thompson • Jacquie Phelan • Janie Eickhoff • Jeanne Golay • Jennie Reed • Juliana Furtado • Margaret Gast • Mari Holden • Mary Jane Reoch • Mildred Kugler • Nancy Burghart Haviland • Nancy Neiman Baranet • Phyllis Harmon • Rebecca Twigg • Robin Morton • Ruthie V Mathes • Sara Ballantyne • Sue Novara Reber • Susan Marie DeMattei • Tillie Anderson

SOURCES

1. Dauncey, Hugh. *French Cycling, A Social and Cultural History*, Liverpool University Press, 2012, page 37.

2. *The Velocepedist*, Feb. 1, 1869. Vol. I, No. 1, page 5.

3. Herlihy, David in email communication with the author, January 14, 2021.

4. Herlihy, David, *The Bicycle*, Yale University Press, 2004, page 136.

5. National Portrait Gallery, npg.org.uk/collections Cora Pearl as Cupid in "Orpheé aux Enfers."

6. Dictionary of National Biography, Ed. Sidney Lee, Vol. XLIV. Paston-Percy.

7. http://collections.domaine-de-sceaux.hauts-de-seine.fr/fr/search-notice/detail/37-1-3-p1617-po-00c89

8. *Leavenworth Times*, Sept. 29, 1869, page 1.

9. *Detroit Free Press*, 11 July 1886, Sunday edition, page 6.

10. *St. Joseph Sunday Herald*, 10 October 1868, page 2.

11. *The Velocipedist*, Vol.1, No. 2, New York, March 1869, page 2.

12. "Editorial Paragraphs, etc.," *The New Orleans Crescent*, 21 March 1869, page 11.

13. "Personal," *Detroit Free Press*, 26 April 1869, pg. 4.

14. "Bicycle Tournament, *The Saint Paul Globe*, 11 Nov. 1883, pg. 2.

15. "New Items," *The Bozeman Weekly Chronicle*, 14 May 1884, page 1.

16. "Jack's Jottings," *Wheelman's Gazette*, June 1889, pg. 95, Vol. 5, No. 6.

17. Robins Pennell, Elizabeth. *Over the Alps on a Bicycle*, T.F. Unwin, Harvard University, 1898, pg. 105.

18. "Female Cyclers Start Today in a Run for the World's Championship," *The Boston Globe*, 11 Feb 1889, pg. 1.

19. "The Girls Are Getting Tired of It," *The Sun*, 13 Feb 1889, pg. 1

20. *The Wheel, A Journal of Cycling*, Vol. VIII, No. 13, pg. 110.

21. "Women on Bicycles: Adaptation of the Two-Wheeled Machine to the use of the Fair Sex," *Boston Globe*, 8 April 1888, pg. 17.

22. Porter, Luther. *Wheels and Wheeling: An Indispensable Handbook for Cyclists*, Boston, Wheelman Company, 1892. Pg. 9.

23. "The Women's Bicycle and Its Predecessor," E.D. Sewall, *The Iron Age*, Vol. 59, May 13, 1897, pg. 8.

24. Willard, Frances E. *A Wheel Within A Wheel: How I Learned to Ride the Bicycle With Some Reflections By the Way*, originally published 1895 by Fleming H. Revell Co., Applewood Books, Bedfield, Mass. 1997, pg. 20.

25. Ibid, pg. 16.

26. Willard, Frances E. *Let Something Good Be Said: Speeches and Writing of Frances E. Willard*. Carol DeSwarte Gifford and Amy R. Slagell, editors. Board of Trustees of the University of Illinois, 2007, page 210.

27. *The Wheel and Cycling Trade Review*, 22 March, 1889, Vol. 3, No. 4, pg. 66.

28. "Fair Bicyclers," *St. Louis Dispatch*, 4 May, 1890, pg. 25.

29. "Their Wheels Spin," *Chicago Tribune*, 15 April 1894, pg. 35.

30. "Woman's World in Paragraphs," *Quad City Times*, 27 Aug 1893, pg. 3.

31. "Bloomers Win," *Seattle Post-Intelligencer*, 5 July 1895, pg. 5.

32. "Cycling in Asbury Park," *The News*, 18 July 1895, pg. 3.

33. *Southern Cycler*, August 1895.

34. De Koven, Mrs. Reginald. "Bicycling for Women," *Cosmopolitan*, August 1895, pg. 386.

35. Ibid, pg. 391.

36. "Woman's Wheeling Dress," *The New York Times*, 23 Dec. 1894, pg. 21.

37. Friss, Evan. *The Cycling City: Bicycles and Urban America in the 1890s*. Chicago, University of Chicago Press, 2015. Pg. 179.

38. Gruber Garvey, Ellen. *The Adman in the Parlor*. USA, Oxford University Press, 1996. Pg. 116.

39. From *Cincinnati Enquirer*, 25 August 1896, quoted via https://www.cincinnatimagazine.com/citywiseblog/no-street-walkers-cincinnati-prostitutes-wheels/

40. *The Buffalo Enquirer*, 27 Feb. 1902, pg. 4.

41. "Has a Famous Record," *Newton Daily Republican*, 11 Feb 1897, pg. 3

42. "Ideal Wheelwoman," *Buffalo Morning Express*, 5 June 1898, pg. 8.

43. "Breaking the Cycle Record, *The Fort Wayne News*, 9 July 1900, pg. 7.

44. "Miss Gast Stopped," *New York Tribune*, 20 October 1900, pg. 5.

45. "Stopped Miss Gast," *Buffalo Morning Express*, 20 October 1900, pg. 12.

46. Bancroft, William. "Colonel Pope and The Bicycle," *Mahin's Magazine*, December, 1902, Vol. 1, No. 9, pg. 18.

47. *Oregon Historical Quarterly*, v. 75, No. 1, March, 1974, pgs 7-35.

48. Jensen, Kimberly. *Oregon's Doctor to the World: Esther Pohl Lovejoy and a Life in Activism*, 2012, University of Washington Press, pg. 51.

49. "Expensive to the Expansive at the Senate," *The Oregonian*, 10 June 1957, pg. 18.

50. Ibid.

51. "The Life and Times of Fred T. Merrill," *Portland Morning Oregonian*, March 15, 1936, pg. 36.

52. "Decease of Biking," *The Times-Democrat*, 30 July 1901, pg. 3.

53. Friss, Evan. Ibid, pg. 190.

54. "Eck Talks of Long Ago," *The Courier-Journal*, 4 Feb. 1906, pg. 34

55. "News of the Bicycle Trade," *The Bicycling World*, supplement to *Motorcycling Illustrated*, May 11, 1916, page 36.

56. Horton, Dave, Rosen, Paul, and Cox, Peter. *Cycling and Society*. 2016, Taylor & Francis, pg. 5.

57. "Taft Had First White House Limo," *St. Petersburg Times*, 11 Nov. 1985, pg. 89.

58. "Why the Ladies Need the Bicycle," *Motorcycle Illustrated*, Vol. 11, No. 7. Pg. 46.

59. Lawrence, Dorothy. *Sapper Dorothy Lawrence*. 1919, London, John Lane, The Bodley Head.

60. "Five New York Girls Go On Bike Trip to the Capitol," *The New York Age*, 14 April 1928, pg. 6.

61. *Dear Scott, Dearest Zelda: The Love Letters of F. Scott and Zelda Fitzgerald*. 2019, Scribner, pg. 210.

62. #39 Turpin, Robert J. *First Taste of Freedom: A Cultural History of Bicycle Marketing in the United States*, Syracuse University Press, 2018. Page 40.

63. "1942 Victory Bicycle" Smithsonian National Museum of American History, https://americanhistory.si.edu/collections/search/object/nmah_1313316

64. from The New York Times *Complete World War II: The Coverage of the Entire Conflict*. Overy, Richard, ed., 2013 Black Dog & Leventhal Publishers. No page numbers.

65. "Hawk Point and Community," *The Warrenton Banner*, 19 Feb. 1942. Pg. 2.

66. "Bicycling Is Studied by Scouts," *Mason City Globe-Gazette*, 19 March 1943, pg. 6.

67. "Bicycle Casualties," *Hygeia*, July, 1946, page 550.

68. "Bicycle Doesn't Beg for Enthusiasm, But Present Risk Is Just Too Much," *The Indianapolis Sunday Star*, 29 March 1942, pg. 8.

69. "Points for Pedalers," The Affiliated Aetna Life Companies, Iowa Department of Safety, 1943. Periscope Film Archive LLC.

70. "Merrily We Roll Along, Yesterday and Now in the Fashion," from Lubbock, Texas *The Sunday Avalanche Journal*, 7 Feb. 1932, page 6.

71. "Style Cycle Complete With Bike Outfits Back," *Courier-Post*, 16 March 1942, pg. 11.

72. "Bicycling Is Tops! Million Fans Join in Year's Pedaling," *The Cincinnati Enquirer*, 16 July 1950, page 2, section 4.

73. Quoted in Turpin, Robert, *First Taste of Freedom*, pg. 174.

74. "Americans Pedal From Ills of Urban Life," *Central New Jersey Home News*, 3 Oct. 1971, pg. D1.

75. "Bike Boom Both Good, Bad for U.S." *The Pittsburgh Press*, 14 May 1973, pg. 15.

76. Ibid, pg. 15.

77. Quoted from Joffrey Nye, Peter. *Hearts of Lions: The History of American Bicycle Racing*. May 2020, University of Nebraska Press. Ch. 12.

78. Ibid.

ABOUT THE AUTHOR

April Streeter writes and bikes from Portland, Oregon. Her career has included five years as correspondent for Sweden, Norway, and the Baltic nations for *Windpower Monthly* magazine, two years as managing editor for *Sustainable Industries* magazine, and many years as correspondent of *Tomorrow* magazine and blogger for TreeHugger. com. She's also on Instagram @womenonwheels.